DATE DUE

APR 20 1983		
FEB 11 1994		
DEC 27 1994		
FEB 10 1995		
APR 3 0 2001		
GAYLORD		PRINTED IN U.S.A.

LECTURES

ON

THE INFLUENCE OF POETRY

AND

WORDSWORTH

LECTURES

ON

THE INFLUENCE OF POETRY

AND

WORDSWORTH

BY

F. W. ROBERTSON

KENNIKAT PRESS
Port Washington, N. Y./London

LECTURES ON THE INFLUENCE OF
POETRY AND WORDSWORTH

First published in 1906
Reissued in 1970 by Kennikat Press
Library of Congress Catalog Card No: 70-105826
ISBN 0-8046-1031-2

Manufactured by Taylor Publishing Company   Dallas, Texas

CONTENTS

PREFACE

IF excuse is needed for the re-appearance of
these three fine interpretations of the true spirit
of poetry by F. W. Robertson, it is surely
promptly found in the quality of the contents,
which the publisher for some time past has
thought should be rescued from the miscel-
laneous volume in which they have hitherto
only been obtainable.

TWO LECTURES ON

THE INFLUENCE OF POETRY

On the Working Classes, delivered before the Members of the Mechanics' Institution, February 1852

LECTURE I *

THE selection of the subject of this evening's Lecture, " The Influence of Poetry on the Working Classes," requires some explanation. What has Poetry to do with the Working Classes? What has it, in fact, to do with this age at all? Does it not belong to the ages past, so that the mere mention of it now is an anachronism—something out of date? Now, there is a large class of persons, to whom all that belongs to our political and social existence seems of such absorbing interest, that they look with impatience on anything which does not bear directly on it. A great political authority of

---

* As some of the topics contained in the following Lectures might seem out of place, as addressed to the members of a Mechanics' Institution, it may be well to state that they were delivered before a mixed audience. They are printed, with some additions, from the corrected notes of a short-hand reporter.

the present day has counselled the young men of this country, and especially of the Working Classes, not to waste their time on literature, but to read the newspapers, which, he says, will give them all the education that is essential. Persons of this class seem to fancy that the all-in-all of man is "to get on"; according to them, to elevate men means, chiefly, to improve their circumstances ; and, no doubt, they would look with infinite contempt on any effort such as this, to interest men on subjects which, most assuredly, will not give them cheaper food or higher wages. " Lecture them," they will say, " on the principles of political economy, in order to stem, if possible, the torrent of those dangerous opinions that threatens the whole fabric of society. Give them, if you will, lectures on science, on chemistry, on mechanics, on any subject which bears on real and actual life ; but, really, in this work-day age, rhyming is out of place and out of date. We have no time for Poetry and prettiness." If, indeed, to have enough to eat and enough to drink were the whole of man—if the highest life consisted in what our American brethren call "going a-head "—if the highest ambition for Working Men were the triumph of some political faction, then, assuredly, the discussion of our present subject would be waste of breath and time.

But it appears to me, that in this age of Mechanics and Political Economy, when every heart seems "dry as summer dust," what we want is, not so much, not half so much—light for the intellect, as dew upon the heart ; time and leisure to cultivate the spirit that is within us.   The author of "Philip Van Artevelde," in his last published volume, "The Eve of the Conquest," has well described this our state of high physical civilization and refinement, in which knowledge is mistaken for wisdom, and all that belongs to man's physical comfort and temporal happiness is sedulously cared for, while much that belongs to our finer and purer being is neglected—an age of grim earnestness —not the noble earnestness of stern Puritanism for high principles, but one which is terrible only when the purse is touched.

"Oh, England ! 'Merry England,' styled of yore !
    Where is thy mirth ?   Thy jocund laughter where ?
    The sweat of labour on the brow of care
Makes a mute answer : driven from every door.
The May-pole cheers the village-green no more,
    Nor harvest-home, nor Christmas mummers rare,
    The tired mechanic at his lecture sighs,
And of the learned, which, with all his lore,
    Has leisure to be wise ? "

Whatever objection may deservedly belong to this Lecture, I hope that no "tired mechanic" will sigh over its tediousness or solemnity.   I believe that recreation is a holy necessity of

man's nature; and it seems to me by no means
unworthy of a sacred calling to bestow an hour
on the attempt to impart not uninstructive recreation to Working Men.

There are some other objections, however,
connected with the subject, which must be
noticed. Poetry may be a fitting study for
men of leisure, but it seems out of the question
for Working Men ;—a luxury for the rich, but
to attempt to interest the poor in it, is as much
out of place as to introduce them into a cabinet
of curiosities, or a gallery of pictures. I believe
such a feeling has arisen partly from this cause
—that the Poetry of the last age was eminently
artificial, unnatural, and aristocratic ; it reflected
the outer life of modern society and its manners,
which are conventional, uniform, polished, and
therefore unnatural, and not of general human
interest. I will read to you a description of
that which one of the poets of that age thought
to be the legitimate call and mission of the poet.
Thus writes Pope :—

" Poetry and criticism are by no means the universal
concern of the world, but only the affair of idle men
who write in their closets, and of idle men who read
there . . .

"All the advantages I can think of, accruing from a
genius for Poetry, are the agreeable power of self-amuse-
ment, when a man is idle or alone ; the privilege of
being admitted into the best company, and the freedom
of saying as many careless things as other people
without being so severely remarked on."

You will scarcely wonder that when a poet could thus write of his art, working men and real men, who have no time for prettinesses, and have not the privilege of being "admitted into the best company," should be indifferent to Poetry, and that it should have come to be reckoned among the luxuries of the wealthy and idle; nor will you be surprised that one who thought so meanly of his high work and duty, should never, with all his splendid talents, have attained to anything in Poetry beyond the second rank, that in which thought and memory predominate over imagination, and in which the heart is second to the head; for much of Pope's Poetry is nothing more than ethical thoughts tersely and beautifully expressed in rhyme.

There is another reason, however, for this misconception. The Poetry of the present age is, to a great extent, touched, tainted if you will, with mysticism. Let us trace the history of this.

A vigorous protest was made at last against the formalism of the Poetry of the last century. The reaction began with Wordsworth, Scott, and Byron, and the age of conventional Poetry was succeeded by the Poetry of sentiment and passion. But, by degrees, this wave also spent itself; and another came. Wordsworth was the poet of the few; the border minstrelsy of Scott

exhausted itself even during his own life; and
when that long, passionate wail of Byronism
had died away,—a phase of tempestuous feeling
through which every man, I suppose, passes in
one portion or other of his existence—men
began to feel that this life of ours was meant
for something higher than for a man to sit
down to rave and curse his destiny; that it is
at least manlier, if it be bad, to make the best
of it, and do what may be done. Next came,
therefore, an age whose motto was "Work."
But now, by degrees, we are beginning to feel
that even work is not all our being needs; and,
therefore, has been born what I have called the
Poetry of Mysticism. For just as the reaction
from the age of Formalism was the Poetry of
Passion, so the reaction from the age of Science
is, and I suppose ever will be, the Poetry of
Mysticism. For men who have felt a want
which work cannot altogether satisfy, and have
become conscious that the clear formulas and
accurate technicalities of science have not expressed, nor ever can, the truths of the Soul,
find a refuge in that vagueness and undefined
sense of mystery which broods over the shape-
less borders of the illimitable. And thus the
very mystic obscurity of thought and expression which belongs to Browning, Tennyson,
and even Wordsworth, is a necessary phase in
the history of Poetry, and is but a protest

and witness for the infinite in the soul of man.

For these two reasons, that the Poetry of the past age was conventional and that of the present mystical, it was very natural that Poetry should have come to be reckoned merely an amusement, suited to men of leisure. But it was not always so : Poetry began, not in the most highly civilized, but in the half-civilized stages of society. The Drama, for example, was first acted in waggons drawn through the Grecian villages, and performed by men who only half-concealed their personality by the rude expedient of smearing the face with the lees of wine. And, before that, the poems of Homer had been recited with enthusiasm in the villages and cities of Ionia, by the people. The poems of Burns, himself a peasant, are the darling favourites of the Scottish peasant, and lie with his Bible, on the same shelf.

And where did our own English Poetry begin, but in those popular ballads of which you have a notable example in the epic ballad of "Chevy Chase"? Poetry is essentially of the people, and for the people.

However, it will be granted, perhaps, that the love of Poetry is compatible with an incomplete education ; but hardly with a want of leisure, or with hard work. To this I reply, first, by a matter of fact : the works of Poetry

in this Institution, since the loss of its first
large library, are few; but those few are largely
read.   Upon the librarian, constant demands
are made for the works of Shakspere and Sir
Walter Scott.

I reply, secondly: I know something myself
of hard work; I know what it is to have had
to toil when the brain was throbbing, the mind
incapable of originating a thought, and the
body worn and sore with exhaustion; and I
know what it is in such an hour, instead of having
recourse to those gross stimulants to which all
worn men, both of the higher and lower classes,
are tempted, to take down my Sophocles or
my Plato (for Plato was a poet), my Goëthe,
or my Dante, Shakspere, Shelley, Wordsworth
or Tennyson; and I know what it is to feel
the jar of nerve gradually cease, and the darkness in which all life had robed itself to the
imagination become light, discord pass into
harmony, and physical exhaustion rise by
degrees into a consciousness of power.   I
cannot, and I will not, believe that this is a
luxury, or rather a blessed privilege, reserved
for me, or my class, or caste, alone.   If I know
from personal experience,—and I do know—
that feelings such as these, call them romantic
if you will, can keep a man all his youth
through, before a higher Faith has been called
into being, from every species of vicious and

low indulgence in every shape and every form,
—if I believe that there are thousands,

> "Whose hearts the holy forms
> Of young imagination have kept pure,"

I am compelled also to believe that, as that
which is human belongs to all humanity, so
there is power in this pursuit to enable the
man of labour to rise sometimes out of his dull,
dry, hard toil, and dreary routine of daily life,
into forgetfulness of his state, to breathe a
higher, and serener, and purer atmosphere. I
will believe that for him, too, there is an

> "Appeal to that imaginative power,
> Which can commute a sentence of sore pain
> For one of softer sadness."

Some years ago, an Irishman, scarcely above
a peasant in rank, was employed on the Ord-
nance Survey, under an officer of Engineers, in
Suffolk, where I then was. I remember the
description he gave me of the state of the Irish
peasantry, and the scenes of wretchedness I
had not then witnessed; "Their cabins, your
honour," said he, "are in such a state sometimes, that the poor craturs could count the
stars as they lay on their beds."

I am not prepared to dispute that it might
have been better for the Irish peasant if, instead
of lying on his bed counting the stars and curs-
ing the Saxon, he had got up and mended his

roof; nor will I enter into the question whether seven hundred years of English misrule have darkened all hope in the nation's breast, and left them neither heart nor spirit to mend and patch a hopeless lot; but I think you will agree with me, that a hard-working man, to whose imagination the thought which spontaneously presented itself on the sight of a roofless hut, was, not that of dripping rain or driving winds, but of poor creatures lying on their beds to count the stars, who could get away from discomfort to expatiate in the skies, was, to some extent, through his imagination and his poetry, independent of external circumstances.

By the title of this Lecture I am bound to define, in the first place, what is meant by "Poetry"; and, in the second, to endeavour to sustain the assertion "that it has a powerful influence on the Working Classes."

The former of these is the subject of this first Lecture. Our first definition of Poetry is—the natural language of excited feeling. When a man is under the influence of some strong emotion, his language, words, demeanour, become more elevated; he is twice the man he was. And not only his words, and posture, and looks, but the whole character and complexion of his thoughts are changed. They belong to a higher order of imagination, and are more full of symbolism, and imagery; the

reason of which is—that all the passions deal
not with the limitations of time and space, but
belong to a world which is infinite.   The strong
passions, whether good or bad, never calculate.
Anger, for example, does not ask for satisfaction
in gold and silver ; it feels and resents a wrong
that is infinite ; Love demands the eternal
blessedness of the thing loved—it feels, and
delights to feel that it is itself infinite, and
can never end ; Revenge is not satisfied with
temporary pain, but imprecates the perdition
of the offender.

And so, these passions of ours, uncalculating,
and outlaws of time and space, disdaining the
bounds of the universe,

" Glancing from heaven to earth, from earth to heaven,"

never argue, but reach at a single bound the
eternal truth, discover unexpected analogies
hidden before through all the universe, and
subordinate each special case to some great
and universal law.

Hence, the language of strong emotion is
always figurative, symbolical, and rich in metaphors.   For the metaphors of Poetry are not
mere ornaments stuck on, and capable of being
taken off without detriment to the essence of the
thought.   They are not what the clothes are to
the body, but what the body is to the life—born
with it ; the form in which the life has been

clothed, without which the life would have been impossible ; just as Minerva is fabled by the ancients to have risen in full panoply out of the brain of Jupiter.

Poetry, I have said, is the *natural* language of excited feeling.   It is not something invented or artificial, but that in which excited feeling naturally clothes itself.   Now take an example. When the Pragmatic Sanction was violated on all sides in Europe, when Silesia had been wrested away by the young King of Prussia, and, with the assistance and sanction of the French, the Elector of Bavaria was aiming at the Crown of the Empire, the Empress Maria Theresa threw herself on her Hungarian sub-jects.   We are told that when, robed in black, she appeared in the Diet, with her child in her arms, and asked their assistance, the Hungarian nobles rose, and, with one voice, exclaimed, " Let us die for our King, Maria Theresa ! " Observe the poetry of the expression, " our *King* Maria Theresa."   No calculation in that moment ; no mercenary sordidness, balancing the question whether a nation could afford to defend weakness and honour at the expense of a costly war, or not.   They had risen in one moment of strong emotion to the highest truth of human existence, the Law of Sacrifice : they had penetrated into that region in which kingly qualities had blended together the two sexes, and broken down the whole barrier of distinction between man and woman; that region in which tenderness and loyalty are not two, but one: "Let us die for our KING, Maria Theresa!"

You will perceive from this that there is an element of poetry in us all. Whatever wakes up intense sensibilities, puts you for a moment into a poetic state; if not the creative state, that in which we can *make* poetry, at least the receptive state in which we *feel* poetry. Therefore, let no man think that, because he cannot appreciate the verse of Milton or Wordsworth, there is no poetry in his soul; let him be assured that there is something within him which may any day awake, break through the crust of his selfishness, and redeem him from a low, mercenary, or sensual existence.

Any man who has for a single moment felt those emotions which are uncalculating, who has ever risked his life for the safety of another, or met some great emergency with unwavering courage, or felt his whole being shaken with mighty and unutterable indignation against some base cruelty or cowardly scoundrelism, knows what I mean when I say that there is something in him which is infinite, and which can transport him in a moment into the same atmosphere which the poet breathes.

"High instincts" Wordsworth calls them

> " Before which our mortal nature
> Did tremble, like a guilty thing surprised :
> . . . . . . those first affections
> Those shadowy recollections
>   Which, be they what they may,
>   Are yet the Fountain-light of all our day,
> Are yet the master-light of all our seeing :
>   Uphold us, cherish, and have power to make
> Our noisy years seem moments in the being
>   Of the Eternal Silence.   Truths that wake
>   To perish never."

Shakspere, who knew all that man can feel, and the times when he feels it, is here, as usual, true to nature. You must have observed that he never puts language highly imaginative, what we call Poetry, into the lips of any except exalted characters, who may be supposed to live in Poetry, or persons who, for the time, are under some exciting influence. If you will compare the manner and expression of Timon of Athens, through the earlier acts, with his language in the latter part of the Play, you will see how he becomes another man under the influence of a powerful passion. At first, you have the high-born, high-bred gentleman, magnificent in his liberality, and princely in his tastes, bestowing a fortune on a dependent whose poverty is the sole bar to a happy marriage, giving away the bay courser to his guest because he admired it ; the munificent patron of the arts, using the conventional

language and the flat, dead politeness of
polished society, with no strong feeling of life,
because nothing has broken the smoothness of
its current. But the shock comes. In temporary reverses he begins to feel the hollowness
of friendship, suspects that men and women are
not what they seem ; and then, with that
passionate scorn which henceforth marks his
character, the real poetry of Timon's existence
begins. And this is made the more remarkable
by the relief in which his character stands out
from the contrast between two misanthropes in
the same Play. One is the generous Timon,
who has despaired of men because he has not
found them what he expected them to be ; the
other, the self-enclosed Apemantus who be-
lieves in the meanness of all human natures
because he is mean himself. Even when the
two reciprocate abuse, the distinction is preserved. Apemantus is merely scurrilous—
"beast" and "toad" are the epithets of his
vocabulary. One pregnant word, alive with
meaning, falls from Timon's lips—" Slave."
And then, disappointed in his best and highest
affections, the whole universe appears to his
disordered imagination overspread with the
guilt of his wrongs : earth and skies and sea
are robbers ; yet his scorn is lofty still : even
gold, the general seducer, he does not curse
with the low invective of the conventicle.

Listen to the impassioned scorner :

"Thou ever young, fresh, lov'd, and delicate wooer,
Whose blush doth thaw the consecrated snow,
That lies on Dian's lap !   Thou visible god,
That solder'st close impossibilities,
And mak'st them kiss !   That speak'st with every
    tongue
To every purpose !   O, thou touch of hearts !"

It is poetry throughout—passion rendered imaginative ; scorn, as contrasted with mere spite.

In saying, however, that Poetry is the language of excited feeling, by excitement is not to be understood mere violence or vehemence : but intensity.   It is with accurate knowledge of human nature that Philip Van Artevelde says to Sir Fleuréant, who is imploring forgiveness with vehement self-reproach : " Thou art a weak, inconstant, violent man." Weakness and violence often go together.   Passion may be violent ; as in the case of Othello, Lear, and Northumberland ; it does not follow that it must : vehemence is simply dependent on physical organization, a mere matter of brain and nerve.   Indeed, the most intense feeling is generally the most subdued and calm : for it is necessarily condensed by repression.   A notable example you have in Wordsworth, the calmest of poets ; so much so, that I have heard him characterised as a Quaker among poets.   And yet he is the author of the sublimest ode in the English language, the Intimations of Immortality from the recollections of childhood. And for his *intensity*, I only appeal to those who have understood his poetry, felt, and loved it.

Yet even in this apparent exception we have a corroboration of the rule. Intense as Wordsworth is, there is in him something wanting for the very highest poetry. He is too calm. There is a want of passion : and hence an entire absence of epic as well as dramatic power ; he reflects when he ought to describe, and describes feeling when he ought to exhibit its manifestation. He sings of our nature as some philosophic spirit might sing of it in passionless realms of contemplation, far away from the discords of actual existence, of a humanity purged and purified, separate from the fierce feelings and wild gusts of passion which agitate real human life. And therefore Wordsworth never can be popular in the true sense of the word. His works will be bought and bound richly, and a few of his poems will be familiar words ; but still he will remain the poet of the few : acknowledged by the many, only because he is reverenced by the few ; those discerning few whose verdict slowly, but surely, leads the world at last.

I have said that Poetry is the natural language of intense feeling. It is in perfect accordance with this that the great master of all criticism, Aristotle, divides Poetry into two orders. He says a poet must be one of two things—a "frenzied man," or an "accomplished man"; in which single sentence are contained whole volumes. There are two kinds of poets; the one inspired, and the other skilful: the one borne away by his own feelings, of which he is scarcely master; the other able rather to conceive feelings and simulate their expression, than possessed by, or possessing them.

Hence it is almost proverbial that the poetic temperament, except in a few cases of felicitously organised constitution, and rare equilibrium of powers, is one of singular irritability of brain and nerve.

Even the placid Wordsworth says—

"We poets in our youth begin with gladness :
But thereof come in the end despondency and madness."

And by this, too, we can understand, and compassionate, I do not say excuse, the force of that temptation of stimulants to which so many gifted natures have fallen a sacrifice. Poetry is the language of excited feeling : properly of pure excitement. But stimulants, like wine, opium, and worse, can produce, or rather simulate, that state of rapturous and ecstatic feeling in which the seer should live ; in which emotions succeed each other swiftly, and imagination works with preternatural power. Hence their seductive power.

Our higher feelings move our animal nature ; and our animal nature, irritated, can call back a semblance of those emotions ; but the whole difference between nobleness and baseness lies in the question whether feeling begins from below or above. The degradation of genius, like the sensualising of passion, takes place when men hope to reproduce, through stimulus of the lower nature, those glorious sensations which it once experienced when vivified from above. Imagination ennobles appetites which in themselves are low, and spiritualises acts which are else only animal. But the pleasures which *begin* in the senses only sensualise.

Burns and Coleridge are the awful beacons to all who feel intensely, and are tempted to re-kindle the vestal flames of genius, when they burn low, with earthly fire.

I give another definition of Poetry. I think I have seen it defined—I am not sure whether I have confounded my own thoughts with what I have a dim recollection of having somewhere read—as " the indirect expression of feelings that cannot be expressed directly." We all have feelings which we cannot express. There is a world into which the poet introduces us, of which the senses are not the organs ; there is a beauty which the eye has never seen, and a music which the ear has never heard. There are truths, eternally, essentially, and necessarily true, which we have never yet seen embodied. And there is, besides, from our human sympathies, a strong necessity for giving utterance to these cravings in us. For language has been given, not merely to make known our own selfish wants, but to impart ourselves to our fellow men. Now, if these intense feelings could be expressed directly, so that when you expressed them, you felt yourself understood as adequately as when you say " I thirst," or " I am hungry," then there would be no Poetry at all ; but, because this is impossible, the soul clothes her intuitions, her aspirations, and forebodings, in those indirect images which she borrows from the material world.

For this reason the earliest language of all nations is Poetry. Language has been truly called fossil Poetry : and just as we apply to domestic use slabs of marble, unconscious almost that they contain the petrifactions of innumerable former lives, so in our every-day language we use the living Poetry of the past, unconscious that our simplest expressions are the fossil forms of feeling which once was vague, and laboured to express itself in the indirect analogies of materialism. Only think from whence came such words as " attention," " understanding," " imagination."

As language becomes more forcible and adequate, and our feelings are conveyed, or supposed
to be conveyed, entirely, Poetry in words becomes more rare. It is then only the deeper
and rarer feelings, as yet unexpressed, which
occupy the poet. Science destroys Poetry :
until the heart bursts into mysticism, and out
of science brings Poetry again ; asserting a
wonder and a vague mystery of life and feeling,
beneath and beyond all science, and proclaiming the wonderfulness and mystery of that
which we seem most familiarly to understand.

I proceed to give you illustrations of this
position, that " Poetry is the indirect expression
of that which cannot be expressed directly."
An American writer tells us that in a certain
town in America there is a statue of a sleeping
boy, which is said to produce a singular feeling
of repose in all who gaze on it ; and the history
of that statue, he says, is this : The sculptor
gazed upon the skies on a summer's morning,
which had arisen as serene and calm as the
blue eternity out of which it came ; he went
about haunted with the memory of that repose
—it was a necessity to him to express it. Had
he been a poet, he would have thrown it into
words ; a painter, it would have found expression on the canvas ; had he been an architect,
he would have given us his feelings embodied
as the builders of the Middle Ages embodied

their aspirations, in a Gothic architecture ; but being a sculptor, his pen was the chisel, his words stone, and so he threw his thoughts into the marble. Now observe, first, this was intense feeling longing to express itself; next, it was intense feeling expressing itself indirectly, direct utterance being denied it. It was not enough to *say*, " I feel repose " ; infinitely more was to be said : more than any words could exhaust : the only material through which he could shape it, and give to airy nothing a body and a form, was the imperfectly expressive material of stone.

From this anecdote we may understand in what sense all the high arts, such as Sculpture, Painting, and Poetry, have been called imitative arts. There was no resemblance between the sleeping boy and a calm morning ; but there was a resemblance between the *feeling* produced by the morning, and that produced by gazing on the statue. And it is in this resemblance between the feeling conceived by the artist, and the feeling produced by his work, that the imitation of Poetry or Art lies. The fruit which we are told was painted by the ancient artist so well that the birds came and pecked at it, and the curtain painted by his rival so like reality that he himself was deceived by it, were imitative so far as clever deception imitates ; but it was not high art, any more than the statue which

many of you saw in the Exhibition last year
was high art, which at a distance seemed
covered with a veil, but on nearer approach
turned out to be mere deceptive resemblance
of the texture, cleverly executed in stone.
This is not the poetry of Art: it is only the
imitation of one species of material in another
species: whereas Poetry is the imitating, by
suggestion through material and form, of
feelings which are immaterial and formless.

Another instance. At Blenheim, the seat of
the Duke of Marlborough, there is a Madonna,
into which the old Catholic painter has tried to
cast the religious conceptions of the Middle
Ages, virgin purity and infinite repose. The
look is upwards, the predominant colour of the
picture blue, which we know has in itself a
strange power to lull and soothe. It is impossible to gaze on this picture without being conscious of a calming influence. During that
period of the year in which the friends of the
young men of Oxford come to visit their
brothers and sons, and Blenheim becomes a
place of favourite resort, I have stood aside,
near that picture, to watch its effect on the
different gazers, and I have seen group after
group of young undergraduates and ladies, full
of life and noisy spirits, unconsciously stilled
before it; the countenance relaxing into calm-
ness, and the voice sinking to a whisper. The

painter had spoken his message, and human beings, ages after, feel what he meant to say.

You may perhaps have seen in this town, some years ago, an engraving in the windows of the printsellers, called the "Camel of the Desert." I cannot say it was well executed. The engraving was coarse, and the drawing, in some points, false ; yet it was full of Poetry. The story tells itself. A caravan has passed through the desert ; one of the number has been seized with dangerous illness, and as time is precious, he has been left to die, but as there is a chance of his recovery, his camel has been left beside him, and in order that it may not escape, the knee of the animal has been forcibly bent, the upper and lower bones tied together, and the camel couched on the ground incapable of rising. The sequel is that the man has died, and the camel is left to its inevitable doom. There is nothing to break the deep deathfulness of the scene. The desert extends to the horizon, without interruption, the glowing heat being shown by the reflection of the sun from the sands in a broad band of light, just as it glows on the sea on a burning summer day.

Nothing, I said, breaks the deathfulness of the scene ; there is only one thing that adds to it. A long line of vultures is seen in the distance, and one of these loathsome birds is hovering above the dead and the doomed ;

the camel bends back his neck to watch it, with an expression of terror and anguish almost human, and anticipates its doom. You cannot look at the print without a vivid sense and conception of Despair. You go through street after street before the impression ceases to haunt you. Had the plate been better executed it is quite possible it might not have been so poetical. The very rudeness and vagueness of it leave much to the imagination. Had the plumage of the vulture, or the hair of the camel more accurately copied the living texture, or the face of the corpse been more death-like, so as, instead of kindling the imagination with the leading idea, to have drawn away the attention to the fidelity with which the accessories had been painted, the Poetry would have been lessened. It is the effort to express a feeling, and the obstacles in the way of the expression, which together constitute the poetical.

Most of us visited the Exhibition in Hyde Park, last year. Some may have seen between the central fountain and the Colebrook Dale gates several cases of stuffed birds, and probably passed on after a customary glance. If so, it was a pity, for there was much Poetry in those cases. They contained a series illustrative of falconry.* In the first case was a gyr-

* Contributed to the Exhibition by Mr Hancock, of Newcastle-upon-Tyne.

falcon, hooded ; in the second, the falcon has
struck his quarry, and the heron lies below with
ruffled crest, and open beak, and writhing, ser-
pentine neck, the falcon meanwhile fixing his
talons deep, and throwing himself backwards
with open wings to avoid the formidable beak.
In the third, the falcon sits gorged upon its
perch.

I have visited the finest museums in Europe,
and spent many a long day in watching the
habits of birds in the woods, hidden and unseen
by them ; but I never saw the reproduction of
life till I saw these. It was not merely the exquisite arrangement of the feathers, nor merely
that the parts which are usually dry and shrunk
in preserved specimens, the beak and the orbits,
the tongue and the legs, were preserved with a
marvellous freshness ; it was not the mere soft-
ness of every swell, and the graceful rise and
bend wherever rise and bend should be, but it
was the life and feeling thrown into the whole,
that dignified these works as real Art. They
were vitalised by the feeling not of the mere
bird-stuffer, but of the poet, who had sympathised with nature, felt the life in birds as
something kindred with his own ; and inspired
with his sympathy, and labouring to utter it,
had thus re-created life as it were within the
very grasp of death.

And while on this subject, I may give you

another illustration, by which you will perceive
the difference between Science and Poetry, in
the works, if you have ever time to read them,
published in a cheap form, of Wilson the
American ornithologist. Wilson was born at
Paisley. His first poetic inspiration came from
the perusal of the works of his countryman,
Burns. He emigrated to America, and there
devoted his life to ornithology. He studied
the life of birds in their native haunts, and the
result was a work which stands amongst the
foremost in its own department, and which one
of the greatest ornithologists of the day, Prince
Lucien Bonaparte, has felt it an honour to
arrange scientifically. Wilson's enthusiasm and
imaginative temperament are manifested in the
singular wish that when he died he might be
buried in the woods, where the birds would sing
above his grave. And all his writing is full of
this living sympathy with life, and poetic power
of perceiving analogies : as when he calls the
Arctic Owl "that great northern Hunter," or
describes the Goat-sucker's discovery of the
robbery of her nest. Whoever has read his
works, or Waterton's Wanderings, or that sweet,
observing description given by Banquo, in
Macbeth, of the swallow's haunts and disposi-
tions, and will compare the aspect in which life
appeared to them with that in which it presents
itself to the mind of the scientific nomenclator,

will understand the different ways in which Intellect and Feeling represent the same objects, and how it is that largeness of sympathy distinguishes poetic sensibility from scientific capacity.   Poetry creates life: Science dissects death.

Our present definition will help to explain why all the scenes of nature are poetic and dear to us.   They express what is in us, and what we cannot express for ourselves.   I love those passages in the Bible which speak of this universe as created by the WORD of God.   For the Word is the expression of the thought; and the visible universe is the Thought of the Eternal, uttered in a word or form in order that it might be intelligible to man.   And for an open heart and a seeing eye it is impossible to gaze on this creation without feeling that there is a Spirit at work, a living WORD endeavouring to make Himself intelligible, *labouring* to express Himself through symbolism and indirect expression, because direct utterance is impossible; partly on account of the inadequacy of the materials, and partly in consequence of the dullness of the heart, to which the infinite Love is speaking.   And thus the word poet obtains its literal significance of maker, and all visible things become to us the chaunted poem of the universe.

These feelings, of course, come upon us most

vividly in what we call the sublime scenes of nature. I wish I could give to the Working Men in this room one conception of what I have seen and witnessed, or bring the emotions of those glorious spots to the hearts of those who cannot afford to see them. I wish I could describe one scene, which is passing before my memory this moment, when I found myself alone in a solitary valley of the Alps, without a guide, and a thunder-storm coming on ; I wish I could explain how every circumstance combined to produce the same feeling, and ministered to unity of impression : the slow, wild wreathing of the vapours round the peaks, concealing their summits, and imparting in semblance their own motion, till each dark mountain form seemed to be mysterious and alive; the eagle-like plunge of the Lämmer-geier, the bearded vulture of the Alps ; the rising of the flock of choughs, which I had surprised at their feast on carrion, with their red beaks and legs, and their wild shrill cries, startling the solitude and silence,—till the blue lightning streamed at last, and the shattering thunder crashed as if the mountains must give way : and then came the feelings, which in their fulness man can feel but once in life ; mingled sensations of awe and triumph, and defiance of danger, pride, rapture, contempt of pain, humbleness and intense repose, as if all the strife and struggle of the elements were only uttering the unrest of man's bosom; so that in all such scenes there is a feeling of relief, and he is tempted to cry out exultingly, There! there! all this was in my heart, and it was never said out till now!

But do not fancy that Poetry belongs to the grander scenes of nature only. The poets have taught us that throughout the whole world there is a significance as deep as that which belongs to the more startling forms, through which Power speaks.

Burns will show you the Poetry of the daisy,

"Wee, modest, crimson-tippèd flower,"

which the plough turns up unmarked; and Tennyson will tell you the significance, and feeling, and meaning there are in the black ash-bud, and the crumpled poppy, and the twinkling laurels, and the lights which glitter on the panes of the gardener's greenhouse, and the moated grange, and the long, grey flats of "unpoetic" Lincolnshire. Read Wordsworth's "Nutting," and his fine analysis of the remorse experienced in early youth at the wanton tearing down of branches, as if the desolation on which the blue sky looks reproachfully through the open space where foliage was before, were a crime against life, and you will feel the intuitive truth of his admonition that "there is a Spirit in the woods."

Nay, even round this Brighton of ours, treeless

and prosaic as people call it, there are materials
enough for Poetry, for the heart that is not
petrified in conventional maxims about beauty.
Enough in its free downs, which are ever chang-
ing their distance and their shape, as the lights
and cloud-shadows sail over them, and over the
graceful forms of whose endless variety of slopes
the eye wanders, unarrested by abruptness, with
an entrancing feeling of fulness, and a restful
satisfaction to the pure sense of Form.   And
enough upon our own sea-shore and in our rare
sunsets.   A man might have watched with delight, beyond all words, last night, the long,
deep purple lines of cloud, edged with intolerable
radiance, passing into orange, yellow, pale green,
and laden blue, and reflected below in warm,
purple shadows, and cold, green lights, upon
the sea—and then, the dying of it all away.
And then he might have remembered those
lines of Shakspere; and often quoted as they
are, the poet would have interpreted the sunset,
and the sunset what the poet meant by the
exclamation which follows the disappearance
of a similar aërial vision—

> "We are such stuff
> As dreams are made of : and our narrow life
> Is rounded with a sleep."

No one has taught us this so earnestly as
Wordsworth; for it was part of his great message
to this century to remind us that the sphere of

the poet is not only in the extraordinary, but
in the ordinary and common.

> " The common things of sky and earth,
>   And hill and valley, he has viewed :
> And impulses of deeper birth
>   Have come to him in solitude.
>
> " From common things, that round us lie,
>   Some random truths he can impart :
> The harvest of a quiet eye,
>   That sleeps and broods on its own heart."

But, of course, if you lead a sensual life, or
a mercenary or artificial life, you will not read
these truths in nature.   The faculty of discerning them is not learnt either in the gin-palace
or the ball-room.   A pure heart, and a simple,
manly life alone can reveal to you all that which
seer and poet saw.

This Lecture will be appropriately closed by
a brief notice of the last work of our chief living
poet, Alfred Tennyson.   And I shall also endeavour to confute certain cavils raised against
it : for after laying down what appear to be the
true canons of criticism, they may be further
substantiated by the exposure of criticism which
is false.

The poem entitled " In Memoriam " is a
monument erected by friendship to the memory
of a gifted son of the historian Hallam.   It is
divided into a number of cabinet-like compart-
ments, which, with fine and delicate shades of

difference, exhibit the various phases through which the bereaved spirit passes from the first shock of despair, dull, hopeless misery and rebellion, up to the dawn of hope, acquiescent trust, and even calm happiness again. In the meanwhile many a question has been solved, which can only suggest itself when suffering forces the soul to front the realities of our mysterious existence ; such as : Is there indeed a life to come ! And if there is, will it be a conscious life ? Shall I know that myself ? Will there be mutual recognition ? continuance of attachments ? Shall friend meet friend, and brother brother, as friends and brothers ? Or, again : How comes it that one so gifted was taken away so early, in the maturity of his powers, just at the moment when they seemed about to become available to mankind ? What means all this, and is there not something wrong ? Is the law of Creation Love indeed ?

By slow degrees, all these doubts, and worse, are answered ; not as a philosopher would answer them, nor as a theologian, or a meta-physician, but as it is the duty of a poet to reply, by intuitive faculty, in strains in which Imagination predominates over Thought and Memory. And one of the manifold beauties of this exquisite poem, and which is another characteristic of true Poetry, is that, piercing through all the sophistries and over-refinements of speculation, and the lifeless scepticism of science, it falls back upon the grand, primary, simple truths of our humanity; those first principles which underlie all creeds, which belong to our earliest childhood, and on which the wisest and best have rested through all ages: that all is right: that darkness shall be clear: that God and Time are the only interpreters: that Love is king: that the Immortal is in us: that—which is the key-note of the whole—

> "all is well, though Faith and Form
> Be sundered in the night of fear."

This is an essential quality of the highest Poetry, whose characteristic is simplicity; not in the sense of being intelligible, like a novel, to every careless reader, without pain or effort: for the best Poetry demands study as severe as mathematics require; and to any one who thinks that it can be treated as a mere relaxation and amusement for an idle hour, this Lecture does not address itself: but simplicity, in the sense of dealing with truths which do not belong to a few fastidious and refined intellects, but are the heritage of the many. The deepest truths are the simplest and the most common.

It is wonderful how generally the formalists have missed their way to the interpretation of this poem. It is sometimes declared with oracular decisiveness, that, if this be Poetry, all they have been accustomed to call Poetry must change its name. As if it were not a law that every original poet must be in a sense new : as if Æschylus were not a poet because he did not write an epic like Homer : or as if the Romantic poets were not poets because they departed from every rule of classical Poetry. And as if, indeed, this very objection had not been brought against the Romantic school, and Shakspere himself pronounced by French critics a " buffoon " : till Schlegel showed that all life makes to itself its own form, and that Shakspere's form had its living laws. So spoke the " Edinburgh Review " of Byron ; but it could not arrest his career. So spoke Byron himself of Wordsworth : but he would be a bold man, or a very flippant one, who would dare to say now that Wordsworth is not a great poet. And the day will come when the slow, sure judgment of Time shall give to Tennyson his undisputed place among the English poets as a true one, of rare merit and originality.

To a coarser class of minds " In Memoriam " appears too melancholy : one long monotone of grief. It is simply one of the most victorious songs that ever poet chanted : with the mysterious undertone, no doubt, of sadness which belongs to all human joy, in front of the mysteries of death and sorrow ; but that

belongs to " Paradise Regained " as well as to
" Paradise Lost ": to every true note, indeed, of
human triumph except a Bacchanalian drinking
song.   And that it should predominate in a
monumental record is not particularly unnatural.   But readers who never dream of
mastering the plan of a work before they pretend to criticise details, can scarcely be expected to perceive that the wail passes into a
hymn of solemn and peaceful beauty before it
closes.

Another objection, proceeding from the
religious periodicals, is, that the subject being
a religious one, is not treated religiously; by
which they mean theologically.   It certainly
is neither saturated with Evangelicalism nor
Tractarianism; nor does it abound in the
routine phrases which, when missed, raise a
suspicion of heterodoxy ; nor does it seize the
happy opportunity afforded for a pious denuncia-
tion of the errors of Purgatory and Mariolatry.
But the objection to its want of definite
theology—an objection, by the way, brought
frequently against Wordsworth by writers of
the same school—is, in fact, in favour of the
presumption of its poetic merit ; for it may be
the office of the priest to teach upon authority
—of the philosopher according to induction—
—but the province of the poet is neither to
teach by induction nor by authority, but to

The Influence of Poetry 43

appeal to those primal intuitions of our being
which are eternally and necessarily true.

With one of those criticisms I mean to occupy
your time at somewhat further length. Some
months ago, a leading journal devoted three
or four columns to the work of depreciating
Tennyson. I will answer that critique now,
as concisely as I can; not because it can do
any permanent harm to Tennyson's reputation,
but because it may do a great deal of harm to
the taste of the readers.

Now, in any pretension to criticise a poetic
work of internal unity, the first duty, plainly,
is to comprehend the structure of it as a whole,
and master the leading idea. It is to be re-
gretted that this is precisely what English
critics generally do not. Even with our own
Shakspere, admiration or blame is usually
confined to the beauties and blemishes of detached passages. For the significance of each
play, as a whole, we had to look, in the first
instance, to such foreigners as Augustus Schlegel
to teach us.

Let us inquire what conception the critic in
question has formed of this beautiful poem.

"Let the acknowledgment be made at once
that the writer dedicated his thoughts to a
most difficult task. He has written 200 pages
upon one person—in other words, he has
painted 120 miniatures of the same individual."

Mr Tennyson has not painted 120 portraits of the same individual. He has written a poem in 120 divisions, illustrative of the manifold phases through which the soul passes from doubt through grief to faith. With so entire and radical a misconception of the scope of the poem, it is not wonderful if the whole examination of the details should be a failure.

The first general charge is one of irreverence. The special case selected is these verses, which are called blasphemous—

> " But brooding on the dear one dead,
>   And all he said of things divine,
>   (And dear as sacramental wine
>   To dying lips is all he said)."

One would have thought that the holy tenderness of this passage would have made this charge impossible. However, as notions of reverence and irreverence in some minds are singularly vague, we will give the flippant objection rather more attention than it merits.

By a sacrament we understand a means of grace: an outward something through which pure and holy feelings are communicated to the soul. In the Church of Christ there are two sacraments—the material of one is the commonest of all elements, water; the form of the other the commonest of all acts, a meal. Now there are two ways in which reverence may be manifested towards any thing or person :

one, by exalting that thing or person by means
of the depreciation of all others ; another, by
exalting all others through it. To some minds
it appears an honouring of the sacraments to
represent them as solitary things in their own
kind, like nothing else, and all other things
and acts profane in comparison of them. It is
my own deep conviction that no greater dis-
honour can be done to them than by this conception, which degrades them to the rank of
charms. The sacraments are honoured when
they consecrate all the things and acts of life.
The commonest of all materials was sanctified
to us in order to vindicate the sacredness of
all materialism, in protest against the false
spiritualism which affects to despise the body,
and the world whose impressions are made
upon the senses ; and in order to declare that
visible world God's, and the organ of His manifestation. The simplest of all acts is sacra-
mental, in order to vindicate God's claim to all
acts, and to proclaim our common life sacred,
in protest against the conception which cleaves
so obstinately to the mind, that religion is the
performance of certain stated acts, not necessarily of moral import, on certain days and in
certain places. If there be anything in this
life sacred, any remembrance filled with sancti-
fying power, any voice which symbolizes to us
the voice of God, it is the recollection of the

pure and holy ones that have been taken from
us, and of their examples and sacred words—

> " dear as sacramental wine
> To dying lips."

In those lines Tennyson has deeply, no doubt
unconsciously, that is, without dogmatic in-
tention, entered into the power of the sacraments to diffuse their meaning beyond themselves.　There is no irreverence in them ; no
blasphemy ; nothing but delicate Christian
truth.

The next definite charge is more difficult to
deal with before a mixed society, because the
shades of the feeling in question blend into
each other with exceeding fine graduation.
The language of the friend towards the departed
friend is represented as unfitted for any but
amatory tenderness.　In this blame the critic
is compelled to include Shakspere : for we all
know that his sonnets, dedicated either to the
Earl of Southampton or the Earl of Pembroke,
contain expressions which have left it a point
of controversy whether they were addressed to
a lady or a friend.　Now in a matter which
concerns the truthfulness of a human feeling,
when an anonymous critic is on one side and
Shakspere on the other, there are some who
might be presumptuous enough to suppose *à
priori* that the modest critic is possibly not the
one in the right.　However, let us examine the

matter. There are two kinds of friendship :
One is the affection of the greater for the less,
the other that of the less for the greater. The
greater and the less may be differences of rank,
or intellect, or character, or power. These are
the two opposites of feeling which respectively
characterise the masculine and the feminine
natures, the familiar symbols of which relation-
ship are the oak and the ivy with its clinging
tendrils. But though they are the masculine
and feminine types, they are not confined to
male and female. Most of us have gone
through both these phases of friendship. Whoever remembers an attachment at school to a
boy feebler than himself, will recollect the
exulting pride of guardianship with which he
shielded his friend from the oppression of some
young tyrant of the playground. And whoever,
at least in boyhood or youth, loved a man, to
whose mental or moral qualities he looked up
with young reverence, will recollect the devotion
and the jealousies, and the almost passionate
tenderness, and the costly gifts, and the desire
of personal sacrifices, which characterise boyish
friendship, and which certainly belong to the
feminine, and not the masculine type of affection. Doubtless the language of "In Memoriam"
is tender in the extreme, such as a sister might
use to a brother deeply loved. But it is to be
remembered that it expresses the affection of

the spirit which rejoices to confess itself the feebler; and besides, that the man has passed into a spirit, and that time and distance have thrown a hallowing haze of tenderness over the lineaments of the friend of the past.   It may be well also to recollect that there is a precedent for this woman-like tenderness, against whose authority one who condemns so severely the most distant approach to irreverence will scarcely venture to appeal.   " I am distressed for thee, my brother Jonathan : very pleasant hast thou been to me.   Thy love to me was wonderful, *passing the love of women.*"

Again, the praise and the grief of the poem are enormously " exaggerated "; and as an instance of the manner in which the "*poet* may underline the moralist," and delicately omit the defects without hyperbolical praise, Dr Johnson's lines on Levett are cited with much fervour of admiration.   Good, excellent Dr Johnson! sincerely pious; very bigoted and very superstitious ; yet one, withal, who fought the battle of life bravely out, in the teeth of disease and poverty; a great lexicographer; of massive learning; the author of innumerable prudential aphorisms, much quoted by persons who season their conversation with proverbs and old saws; the inditer of several thousand ponderous verses; a man worthy of all respect.   But it is indeed a surprising apparition when the

shade of Dr Johnson descends upon the Nine-
teenth Century as the spirit of a poet, and
we are asked to identify the rugged portrait
which Boswell painted, with a model of delicate
forbearance.

After these general observations, the writer
proceeds to criticise in detail : he awards some
praise, and much blame. You shall have a
specimen of each. Let us test the value of his
praise. He selects for approbation, among
others, these lines :—

> " Or is it that the Past will win
> A glory from its being far ;
> And orb into the perfect star
> We saw not when we moved therein !"

The question has suggested itself as a mis-
giving to the poet's mind, whether his past
affection was really as full of blessedness as
memory painted it, or whether it be not the
perspective of distance which conceals its im-
perfections, and throws purer hues upon it than
it possessed while actual. In the rapid reading
of the last two lines I may not have at once
conveyed to you the meaning. So long as we
remain upon any planet, this earth for instance,
it would wear a common-place, earthly look :
but if we could ascend from it into space, in
proportion to the distance, it would assume a
heavenly aspect, and orb or round itself into
a star. This is a very simple and graceful

illustration.   Now hear the critic condescending
to be an analyst of its beauties :

"There is indeed something striking and
suggestive in comparing the gone by time to
some luminous body rising like a red harvest
moon behind us, lighting our path homeward."

So that this beautiful simile of Tennyson's, of
a distant star receding into pale and perfect
loveliness, in the hands of the critic becomes *a
great red harvest moon !*

So much for the praise.   Now for the blame.
The following passage is selected :—

> "Oh, if indeed that eye foresee,
>   Or see (in Him is no before)
>   In more of life true love no more,
> And love the indifference to be,
>
> "So might I find, ere yet the morn
>   Breaks hither over Indian seas,
>   That Shadow waiting with the keys,
> To cloak me from my proper scorn."

That is, as you will see at once, after the
thought of the transitoriness of human affection has occurred to him, the possibility is also
suggested with it, that he himself may change ;
but he prays that before that day can come, he
may find the Shadow waiting with the keys to
cloak him from his own scorn.   Now I will
read the commentary :—

"Lately we have heard much of keys, both
from the Flaminian Gate and Piccadilly, but

we back this verse against Hobbs. We dare
him to pick it. Mr Moxon may hang it up in
his window, with a 200*l.* prize attached, more
safely than a Brahmah. That a shadow should
hold keys at all, is a noticeable circumstance;
but that it should wait with a cloak, ready to
be thrown over a gentleman in difficulties, is
absolutely amazing."

The lock may be picked without any exer-
tion of unfair force.

A few pages before he has spoken of the
breaking up of a happy friendship—

> " There sat the Shadow, feared by man,
>   Who broke our fair companionship."

Afterwards he calls it :—

> " The Shadow, cloaked from head to foot,
>   Who keeps the key of all the creeds."

Take, at a venture, any charity-school boy,
of ordinary intelligence; read to him these
lines; and he will tell you that the Shadow
feared by man is death; that it is cloaked from
head to foot because death is mysterious, and
its form not distinguishable; and that he keeps
the keys of all the creeds, because he alone can
unlock the secret of the grave, and show which
of all conflicting human creeds is true.

" It is a noticeable thing," we are told, " that
a shadow should hold keys at all." It is a very
noticeable thing that a skeleton should hold

a scythe and an hour-glass : very noticeable
that a young lady should hold scales when she
is blind-fold ; yet it is not a particularly un-
common rule of symbolism so to represent
Time and Justice. Probably the writer in the
criticism, if he should chance to read of " riding
on the wings of the wind," would consider
it a very noticeable method of locomotion ;
perhaps would inquire, with dull facetiousness,
what was the precise length of the primary,
secondary, and tertiary quills of the said wings ;
and if told of a spirit clothing itself in light, he
might triumphantly demand in what loom light
could be woven into a greatcoat.

Finally. The critique complains that a vast
deal of poetic feeling has been wasted on a
lawyer ; and much wit is spent upon the tenderness which is given to " Amaryllis of the
Chancery bar." A barrister, it seems, is beyond
the pale of excusable, because poetical sensibilities. So that, if my friend be a soldier, I
may love him, and celebrate him in poetry,
because the profession of arms is by all conventional associations heroic : or if he bears on
his escutcheon the red hand of knighthood, or
wears a ducal coronet, or even be a shepherd,
still there are poetic precedents for romance ;
but if he be a member of the Chancery bar, or
only a cotton lord, then, because these are not
yet grades accredited as heroic in song, worth

is not worth, and honour is not honour, and
nobleness is not nobility. O, if we wanted
poets for nothing else, it would be for this, that
they are the grand levellers, vindicating the
sacredness of our common humanity, and in
protest against such downright vulgarity of
heart as this, reminding us that—

> " For a' that, and a' that,
> A man's a man for a' that."

So much then for this critic : wrong when
he praises and wrong when he blames : who
finds Shakspere false to the facts of human
nature, and quotes Dr Johnson as a model
poet : who cannot believe in the Poetry of any
expression unless it bear the mint stamp of
a precedent, and cannot understand either the
exaggerations or the infinitude of genuine grief.

Let it serve to the members of this Institution
as a comment on the opinion quoted at the
outset, that it is sufficient education for Working Men to read the newspapers. If they form
no more living conception of what Poetry is
than such as they get from the flippant criticism
of a slashing article, they may learn satire, but
not enthusiasm. If they limit their politics to
the knowledge they may pick up from daily
newspapers (which, with a few honourable
exceptions, seem bound to pander to all the
passions and prejudices of their respective

factions) they will settle down into miserable partizans. And if Working Men are to gain their notions of Christianity from the sneering, snarling gossip of the religious newspapers, I for one, do not marvel that indignant infidelity is so common amongst them.

And let it be to us all a warning against that detracting, depreciating spirit which is the curse and bane both of the religion and the literature of our day—that spirit which has no sympathy with aught that is great beyond the pale of customary formalities, and sheds its blighting influence over all that is enthusiastic, and generous, and high-minded. It is possible for a sneer or a cavil to strike sometimes a superficial fact ; I never knew the one or the other reach the deep heart and blessedness of truth.

LECTURE II

In the former Lecture I endeavoured to answer the question—What is Poetry? Two replies were given: It is the natural language of excited feeling; and—A work of imagination wrought into form by art. We said that it arises out of the necessity of expression, and the impossibility of adequate expression of any of the deeper feelings in direct terms. Hence the soul clothes those feelings in symbolic and sensuous imagery, in order to *suggest* them.

And thus our definitions agree with two of Milton's requirements for Poetry—that it be "simple, sensuous, passionate." Sensuous, that is, suggestive to the imagination of truth through images which make their impression on the senses. Passionate, that is, as opposed to scientific; for the province of Poetry is not the intellect, but the feelings.

And thus, too, they coincide with the character given to Poetry by the great critic of antiquity, as an imitative art: for it is the art of suggesting and thus imitating through form, the feelings that have been suggested by another form, or perhaps have arisen without form at all.   So it takes its place with all art, whose office is not to copy form by form, but to express and hint spiritual truths.

It is plain, from what has been said, that Poetry may be spoken of in two senses.   In the specific or technical sense, by Poetry we mean the expression in words, most appropriately metrical words, of the truths of imagination and feeling.   But in the generic and larger sense, Poetry is the expression of imaginative truth in any form, provided only that it be symbolic, suggestive, and indirect.   Hence we said that there is a Poetry of sculpture, architecture, painting; and hence all nature is poetical, because it is the form in which the eternal Feeling has clothed itself with infinite suggestiveness : and hence Lord Byron calls the stars " the Poetry of heaven " ; and tells us that to him " high mountains were a feeling " ; and that mountain and wood and sky spake

" A mutual language, clearer than the tome
   Of his land's tongue, which he would oft forsake
   For Nature's pages, glassed by sunbeams on the lake."

And hence Wordsworth tells us that Liberty has two voices :

"One is of the sea,
And one is of the mountains."

And hence a greater than either has said that the Heavens speak, and that " There is neither speech nor language where their voices are not heard." And hence, too, Woman has been called the Poetry of life, because her presence in this lower world expresses for us, as well as calls out, those infinite feelings of purity, tenderness, and devotion, whose real existence is in our own bosoms. And hence, again, there is a Poetry in music: not in that in which sound imitates sound, as when the roaring of the sea, or the pattering of the rain, or church bells, or bugles, or the groans of the dying are produced, for in such cases there is only a mimicry, more or less ingenious; but that in which we can almost fancy that there is something analogous to the inner history of the human heart,—an expression of resolve or moral victory, or aspiration, or other feelings far more shadowy, infinite, and intangible: or that in which the feelings of a nation have found for themselves an indirect and almost unconscious utterance, as it is said of the Irish melody, that through it, long centuries of depression have breathed themselves out in cadences of a wild, low wail.

We divided poets into two orders: those in whom the vision and the faculty divine of imagination exists; and those in whom the plastic power of shaping predominates;—the men of poetic inspiration, and the men of poetic taste. In the first order I placed Tennyson; in the second, Pope.

Considerable discussion, I am told, has been excited among the men of this Institution by both these positions,—some warmly defending them, and others as warmly impugning. For myself, it is an abundant reward to find that Working Men can be interested in such questions;—that they can debate the question whether Pope was a poet, and be induced to read Tennyson. For the true aim of every one who aspires to be a teacher is, or ought to be, not to impart his own opinions, but to kindle other minds. I care very little, comparatively, whether you adopt my views or not ; but I do care much to know that I can be the humble instrument, in this or higher matters, of leading any man to stir up the power within him, and to form a creed and faith which are in a living way, and not on mere authority, his own.

However, I will explain to you on what grounds I made these two assertions. And, first, as respects Pope—if any one approved of what I said, under the impression that I denied to Pope the name of poet, I must disclaim his approbation : I did not say so. Pope is a true poet : in his own order he stands amongst the foremost ; only, that order is the second, not the first. In the mastery of his materials, which are words, in the plastic power of expression, he is scarcely surpassed. His melody

—I do not say his harmony, which is a much higher thing—is unquestionable. There is no writer from whom so many of those sparkling, epigrammatic sentences, which are the staple commodities of quotation, are introduced into conversation : none who can be read with more pleasure, and even profit. He has always a masculine fancy; more rarely, imagination. But you look in vain for the truths which come from a large heart and a seeing eye; in vain for the "thoughts that breathe and the words that burn"; in vain for those flashes of truth, which, like the lightning in a dark night, make all luminous, open out unsuspected glories of tree and sky and building, interpret us to ourselves, and "body forth the shapes of things unknown": truths which are almost prophetic. Who has not read his Essay on Man, again and again? And yet it is but the philosophy of Bolingbroke, melodiously expressed in rhyme: whereas the office of Poetry is not to make us think accurately, but feel truly. And his Rape of the Lock, which seems to me the one of all his works that most deserves the name of Poetry, the nearest approach to a creation of the fancy, describes aristocratic society, which is uniform, polished, artificial, and out of which a mightier master of the art than Pope could scarcely have struck the notes of true passion. Moreover, its

·machinery, the Rosicrucian fancies of sylphs and gnomes, is but machinery, lifeless. If you compare Shakspere's Ariel or Puck, things alive, preternatural, and yet how natural! with these automatons, you will feel the difference between a living creation and cleverly moved puppet work. Throughout you have thought, not imagination : intellect, not intuition.

I read you last time Pope's estimate of his own art ; now, contrast it with the conceptions formed of Poetry by men whom I would place in the first order.

First, let Burns speak. The spirit of Scottish poesy has appeared to him, and given him his commission.   She says—

> " I saw thee seek the sounding shore,
> Delighted with the dashing roar ;
> Or when the North his fleecy store
> Drove thro' the sky,—
> I saw grim Nature's visage hoar,
> Struck thy young eye.
>
> " Or when the deep, green-mantled earth,
> Warm-cherish'd ev'ry flow'ret's birth,
> And joy and music pouring forth
> In ev'ry grove,—
> I saw thee eye the gen'ral mirth,
> With boundless love."

Observe that exquisite account of the true poetic or creative power, which comes from love, the power of sympathy with the happi-

ness of all kinds of being—"I saw thee eye
the general mirth *with boundless love !*"

Wordsworth shall speak next. I select his
Sonnet to Haydon. You remember poor
Haydon's tragic end. He died by his own
hand, disappointed because the world had not
appreciated nor understood his paintings. It
had been well for Haydon had he taken to
heart the lesson of these lines, pregnant with
manly strength for every one, poet or teacher,
who is striving to express deep truths for
which the men of his generation are not
prepared.

And remark, merely by the way, in this
sonnet, Wordsworth's corroboration of the view
I have placed before you, that Poetry is a something to which words are the accidental, not by
any means the essential form.

> "High is our calling, friend ! Creative Art,
> (Whether the instrument of words she use,
> Or pencil pregnant with ethereal hues,)
> Demands the service of a mind and heart,
> Though sensitive, yet, in their weakest part,
> Heroically fashioned—to infuse
> Faith in the whispers of the lonely Muse,
> While the whole world seems adverse to desert.
> And, oh ! when Nature sinks, as oft she may,
> Through long-lived pressure of obscure distress,
> Still to be strenuous for the bright reward,
> And in the soul admit of no decay,
> Brook no continuance of weak-mindedness—
> Great is the glory, for the strife is hard !"

We will next listen to the account given us by Milton, of the conditions under which Poetry is possible,—lofty and majestic, as we should expect from him :—

" This is not to be obtained but by devout prayer to that Eternal Spirit that can enrich with all utterance and knowledge, and sends his seraphim with the hallowed fire of his altar, to touch and purify the lips of whom he pleases.   To this must be added industrious and select reading, steady observation, and insight into all seemly and generous acts and affairs."

Tennyson shall close this brief list, with what he thinks the poet's calling :

> " The poet in a golden clime was born,
>   With golden stars above ;
>   Dower'd with the hate of hate, the scorn of scorn,
>   The love of love."

That is,—the Prophet of Truth receives for his dower the scorn of men in whose breasts scorn dwells ; hatred from men who hate ; while his reward is in the gratitude and affection of men who seek the truth which they love, more eagerly than the faults which their acuteness can blame.

> " He saw through life and death, thro' good and ill,
>   He saw thro' his own soul,
>   The marvel of the everlasting will,
>   An open scroll,
>
> " Before him lay."

And again :

> " Thus truth was multiplied on truth : the world
>   Like one great garden show'd,
> And thro' the wreaths of floating dark upcurled
>   Rare sunrise flow'd.

> "And Freedom rear'd in that august sunrise,
>   Her beautiful, bold brow,
> When rites and forms before his burning eyes
>   Melted like snow."

Rare gifts of nature : power to read the " open
secret of the universe " ; the apostleship of light,
truth, liberty : the faculty of discerning the life
and meaning which underlie all forms : this is
Tennyson's notion of a poet. You have heard
the master-spirits discoursing of their art. Now
if after these, you turn to Pope's conception
again, you will feel there is a descent as into
another region. A mighty gulf lies between.
It is impossible to place these men in the same
order. No man is higher than his own ideal of
excellence ; it is well if he attains that. Pope
reached all he aimed at : he reached no more.

I placed Tennyson in the first order. And
this not from any bigoted blindness to his
deficiencies and faults, which are many ; nor
from any Quixotic desire to compare him with
the very highest ; but because, if the division
be a true one which separates poets into the
men of genuine passion and men of skill, it is
impossible to hesitate in which Tennyson is to

be placed. I ranked him with the first order, because with great mastery over his material; words, great plastic power of versification and a rare gift of harmony, he has also Vision or Insight; and because, feeling intensely the great questions of his day, not as a mere man of letters but as a man, he is to some extent the interpreter of his age, not only in its mysticism, which I tried to show you is the necessary reaction from the rigid formulas of science and the earthliness of an age of work, into the vagueness which belongs to infinitude, but also in his poetic and almost prophetic solution of some of its great questions.

Thus in his Princess, which he calls a "medley," the former half of which is sportive, and the plot almost too fantastic and impossible for criticism, while the latter portion seems too serious for a story so slight and flimsy, he has with exquisite taste disposed of the question which has its burlesque and comic as well as its tragic side, of woman's present place and future destinies. And if any one wishes to see this subject treated with a masterly and delicate hand, in protest alike against the theories which would make her as the man, which she could only be by becoming masculine, not manly, and those which would have her to remain the toy, or the slave, or the slight thing of sentimental and frivolous accomplishment which education has hitherto aimed at making her, I would recommend him to study the last few pages of the Princess, where the poet brings the question back, as a poet should, to nature ; develops the ideal out of the actual woman, and reads out of what she is, on the one hand, what her Creator intended her to be, and, on the other, what she never can nor ought to be.

And again, in his " In Memoriam," he has grappled with the scepticism of his age ; not like the school-divine, but like a poet ; not as a priest, with the thunder of the pulpit, or the ban of the conventicle, but as a man : a man of large, human heart, who feels that not doubt, but faith is greatness and blessedness, yet that doubt must not be put down by force or terror, nor silenced by logic, but pass into belief through sorrow, and by appeal to the intuitions of the Soul.

The severity with which an article written against this poem was criticised in the previous lecture, may have seemed to you more than adequate. Let me explain. Three things only in this world should receive no quarter : Hypocrisy, Pharisaism, and Tyranny. Hypocrisy, of course, is out of the question here. But by Pharisaism in religion, we mean, not attachment to forms, but an incapacity of seeing or believing in goodness separate from some particular form, either of words or ritual.

The incipient stage of Pharisaism is that in which men are blind to excellence which does not belong to their own faction : the final and completed stage is that in which goodness seems actually evil.   Plainly, there can be no remedy for that : when good is taken for evil, and evil for good, the heart has reached its last rottenness. By Pharisaism in art we mean, not an attachment to particular schools, but an inability of recognising beauty, except in accordance with conventional rules and established maxims : its incipient stage is when beauty in aberrant types is not felt; its final and hopeless stage is reached when such beauty appears deformity.

Now it was the Pharisaism of that article which appeared to me to deserve no common severity.

Tyranny merits the same treatment.   Had it been from a feeble antagonist that this criticism proceeded, it might have been left unnoticed. Who "breaks a butterfly upon a wheel"?   Or had it been vulgar, personal slander, it had been met, as all such things are best met, in silence.   But the journal in which this critique appeared is no vulgar slanderer ; scarcely ever is an article in its columns deficient in talent at least ; few would like to writhe beneath its lash. It wields a gigantic power.   Well, it is excellent

"To have a giant's strength : but it is tyrannous
    To use it like a giant."

And because that article was written with
merciless severity, weighted with all the
authority of a powerful journal, and hidden
behind the shelter of an anonymous incognito,
therefore it seemed to me a bounden duty to
show to Working Men that a giant can be
crushed, and that they are not to be led
blindfold by the press ; inasmuch as even an
article in the "leading journal of Europe"
may be flippant, clever, arrogant, and
shallow.

We proceed to the more direct business of
this evening : the *influence* of Poetry on the
Working Classes. But first, I disclaim the
notion of treating this subject as if Poetry had
a different sort of influence on them from that
which it has on other classes. Very false is
that mode of thought which recognises the souls
of the classes who are not compelled to work as
composed of porcelain, and of those who are
doomed to work as made of clay. They feel,
weep, laugh, alike : alike have their aspiring
and their degraded moods : that which tells on
one human spirit, tells also upon another.
Much, therefore, of what is to be said will belong to men of work ; not especially, but only
as human beings. If Poetry influences men, it
must influence Working Men.

The influence of Poetry depends partly on
the form ; and partly on the spirit which

animates the form.   I will consider the influence of form first.

We have defined Poetry to be a work of imagination wrought into form by art.   Poetry is not imagination, but imagination shaped. Not feeling; but feeling expressed symbolically: the formless suggested indirectly through form.   Hence the form is an essential element of Poetry; and it becomes necessary to trace its influence.

The form in which political feeling expresses itself is infinitely varied.   There may be a poetical act, or a poetical picture, or a poetical aspect of scenery, or poetical words; to which last form we technically give the name of Poetry.

Take an example from an expression of countenance, which may be poetical.   There are feelings which cannot be spoken out in words; therefore the Creator has so constituted the human countenance that it is expressive, and you only catch the meaning sympathetically by the symbolism of the features.   We have all seen such Poetry.   We have seen looks inspired. We have seen whole worlds of feeling in a glance; scorn, hatred, devotion, infinite tenderness.   This is what, in portraits, we call expression, as distinguished from similarity of feature.   Innumerable touches perfect the one: sometimes one masterly stroke will suggest the

other, so that nothing can add to it. This is
Poetry. To such a look the addition of a word
would have spoilt all—

> "For words are weak, and most to seek,
>   When wanted fifty-fold ;
> And then, if silence will not speak,
> And trembling lip, and changing cheek,
>   There's nothing *told*."

The form of Poetry, again, may be that of a
symbolical action. The Eastern nations express
themselves abundantly in this way : and if the
subject were not too sacred, I might adduce
many examples from the significant actions
of the Hebrew prophets. But I will, instead,
instance a case of modern history. Perhaps
you have read the ancedote (I do not know on
what historical authority it rests) of the Earl of
Warwick, in one of his last battles, probably
that of Barnet, when he found the day going
against him, dismounting from his favourite
charger, and before all his army plunging his
sword into its heart, thereby cutting off the
possibility of escape, and expressing his resolve
there to win or fall. Conceive Warwick putting
that into direct words. Conceive his attempt-
ing to express all that was implied in that act :
the energy of despair, the resolve, the infinite
defiance, the untold worlds of *force* that must
be in a man who could do an act the whole
terribleness of which none but a soldier could

appreciate, slaying with his own hand the horse and friend that had borne him through death and perils. And conceive the influence upon the troops—how it must have said to any recreant waverer in the ranks, "Stand like a man, and dare to die!"

The next instance is a less dignified one ; but I select it that we may discern the manifold shapes and degrees of poetic form. History tells us of a prince of France who asked permission to offer a present to one much loved. The permission was given : the gift chosen, a portrait : but with a stipulation annexed, in order to prevent extravagance, that it should not be larger than could be worn as a ring upon the finger, and that it should not be set in jewels. The portrait was completed as agreed on ; but, instead of a glass, it was covered with a single plate, cut out of the centre of an enormous diamond, which, of course, was sacrificed in the cutting. When the ingenious treachery was discovered, the picture was returned : whereupon the royal lover ground the diamond to powder, and dusted with it, instead of sand, his letter of reply. The use of this ? It was useless. Had it been a matter of utility, it had not been one of Poetry. It was modified by French feeling, doubtless. Yet beneath it you will discern something that was not merely French, but human, and which constitutes the

Poetry of the whole system of present giving. That which in the polite Frenchman was something more than gallantry, would have been in another, and in him, too, under more earnest or less successful circumstances, the chivalrous feeling which desires to express itself in its true essence, as devotion to the weaker, through a sacrifice which shall be costly (the costlier the more grateful, as the relief of feeling to the giver), and which shall be quite immeasurable by, and independent of, the question of utility. The love of the base and plebeian spirit is the desire to *take* all it can. The love of the nobler spirit is the desire to *give* all it can. Sacrifice is its only true expression ; and every form of sacrifice in which the soul tries to express and relieve itself, whether it be in the lavish magnificence in which self and life can be freely spent, or the vulgar magnificence called princely, with which gold and jewels can be squandered, is a form of Poetry, more or less dignified.

It will now be clear, that in the large sense of the word Poetry, its proper form is always symbolism. The poet derives his power from the ardour of mankind to adopt symbols, and catch enthusiasm from them. Poetry is the language of symbolism.

Therefore we all are susceptible of its influences. Many a man who thinks he has no taste for Poetry, because he does not chance to feel it in one of its forms, rhythmic words, is yet no stranger to its power. What is religious formalism, but an exaggeration or petrifaction of a true conviction—that outward forms and material symbols have a language of their own, fraught with a deeper, because infinite, religious significance to the heart than ever came from the poor rhetoric of the pulpit? Why is it that on the battlefield there is ever one spot where the sabres glitter faster, and the pistol's flash is more frequent, and men and officers crowd together in denser masses? They are struggling for a flag, or an eagle, or a standard. Strip it of its symbolism—take from it the meaning with which the imagination has invested it, and it is nothing but a bit of silk rag, torn with shot and blackened with powder. Now go with your common sense and tell the soldier he is madly striving about a bit of rag. See if your common sense is as true to him as his Poetry, or able to quench it for a moment.

Take a case. Among the exploits of marvellous and almost legendary valour performed by that great Chieftain, to whom not many years ago, when disaster after disaster left it uncertain whether the next mail would brings us news that we possessed any Indian Empire at all, the voice of England, with one unanimous impulse, cried, "There is one man in Britain who has the right of wisdom as well

as courage to command in chief,"—that daring
warrior who, when the hour of danger was
past, and the hour of safety had come, was
forgotten by his country ; to whom in the hour
of fresh danger the people of England will
look again, and his generous spirit will forget
neglect ; who has been laid aside uncoroneted
and almost unhonoured, because he *would* pro-
mote and distinguish the men of work in preference to the men of rank, and wealth, and
titled idleness—amongst his achievements not
the least wondrous was his subjugation of the
robber tribes of the Cutchee hills, in the North
of Scinde. Those warriors had been unsubdued
for six hundred years. They dwelt in a crater-
like valley, surrounded by mountains, through
which there were but two or three narrow entrances, and up which there was no access but by
goat paths, so precipitous that brave men grew
dizzy and could not proceed. So rude and
wild was the fastness of Trukkee, that the
entrances themselves could scarcely be discovered amidst the labyrinth-like confusion of
rocks and mountains. It was part of the
masterly plan by which Sir Charles Napier had
resolved to storm the stronghold of the robbers,
to cause a detachment of his army to scale the
mountain side. A service so perilous could
scarcely be commanded. Volunteers were
called for. There was a regiment, the 64th

Bengal Infantry, which had been recently dis-
graced, in consequence of mutiny at Shikarpoor,
their colonel cashiered, and their colours taken
from them—a hundred of these men volunteered.
"Soldiers of the 64th," said the commander,
who knew the way to the soldier's heart, "your
colours are on the top of yonder hill!" I
should like to have seen the precipice that
would have deterred the 64th regiment, after
words like those from the lips of the conqueror
of Scinde!

And now, suppose that you had gone with
common-sense and economic science, and proved
to them that the colours they were risking their
lives to win back, were worth but so many
shillings sterling value—tell me, which would
the stern workers of the 64th regiment have
found it easiest to understand, common-sense
or Poetry? Which would they have believed,
Science, which said, " It is manufactured silk ";
or Imagination, whose kingly voice had made it
"colours"?

It is in this sense that the poet has been
called as the name imports, creator, namer,
maker. He stamps his own feeling on a form
or symbol: names it, and makes it what it was
not before: giving to feeling a local habitation
and a name, by associating it with form. Before, it was silk—so many square feet: now, it
is a thing for which men will die.

And here we get at two distinctions—

First, between the poet and the rhymester. A poet is one who creates or names : who interprets old or new thoughts by fresh symbolism. The rhymester repeats the accredited forms and phrases : and because he has got the knack of using metaphors and diction, which have been the living language of the makers of them, he is mistaken for a poet. Smooth writing, and facility of versification, and expertness in piecing together poetical words and images, do not constitute Poetry.

Next, a distinction between the poet and the mystic. The poet uses symbols, knowing that they are symbols. The mystic mistakes them for realities. Thus to Swedenborg a cloud, or a vine, or a cedar, correspond throughout Scripture with one mystic spiritual truth ; mean one thing, and but one. And thus to the mystical formalist, a sign or symbol is confused with the truth which it symbolises : that symbol is *the* symbol of that truth : and to treat the symbol as Hezekiah treated the brazen serpent is sacrilege. Now, the poet remains sane upon this point : his " fine frenzy " never reaches the insanity which mistakes his own creations for fixed realities. To him a cloud or flower may express at different times a thousand truths : material things are types to him, in a certain mood, of this truth or that ; but he knows that

to another person, or to himself in another
mood, they are types of something else.

Tennyson has said this well—

"But any man who walks the mead,
    In bud, or blade, or bloom may find,
According as his humours lead,
    A meaning suited to his mind.
For liberal applications lie
    In Art as Nature, dearest friend :
So 'twere to cramp its use, if I
    Should hook it to some useful end."

And this will help us to discern how far there
is truth in the opinion that Poetry belongs to
the earlier ages, and declines with the advance
of civilization.   Symbols perish—Poetry never
dies.   There was a time when the Trojan war,
before Homer sang it, was what Milton says of
the unsung wars of the Saxon Heptarchy, a
conflict of kites and crows ; the martyr's stake,
a gibbet ; Olympus and Parnassus, and a hill
more holy still, common hills.   The time may
come when, as they were once without poetical
associations, most of them shall be unpoetical
again.   And because of such a dying of the
glory from the past, people begin to fancy that
Poetry has perished.   But is human courage
lost, fidelity, imagination, honourable aims ?   Is
the necessity of utterance gone, or the suffi-
ciency of finite words for illimitable feeling
greater ?   When the old colours of a regiment

are worn out, it is sometimes the custom to burn them, and drink the ashes in wine, with solemn silence : before the consecration of new colours. Well, that is all we want. Let old forms and time-honoured words perish with due honour, and give us fresh symbols and new forms of speech to express, not what our fathers felt, but what we feel. Goëthe says, " The spirit-world is not foreclosed. *Thy* senses are dulled ; *thy* heart is dead. Arise, become a learner ; and bathe that earthly breast of thine, unwearied, in the dew of a fresh morning."

And this alone would be enough to show that the Poetry of the coming age must come from the Working Classes. In the upper ranks, Poetry, so far at least as it represents their life, has long been worn out, sickly, and sentimental. Its manhood is effete. Feudal aristocracy with its associations, the castle and the tournament, has passed away. Its last healthy tones came from the harp of Scott. Byron sang its funèral dirge. But tenderness, and heroism, and endurance still want their voice, and it must come from the classes whose observation is at first hand, and who speak fresh from nature's heart. What has Poetry to do with the Working Classes ? Men of work ! we want our Poetry from you—from men who will dare to live a brave and true life ; not like poor Burns, who was fevered with flattery, manful as he was, and dazzled by the vulgar splendours of the life of the great, which he despised and still longed for ; but rather like Ebenezer Elliot, author of the Corn Law Rhymes.   Our soldier ancestors told you the significance of high devotion and loyalty which lay beneath the smoke of battle-fields.   Now rise and tell us the living meaning there may be in the smoke of manufactories, and the heroism of perseverance, and the poetry of invention, and the patience of uncomplaining resignation.   Remember the stirring words of one of your own poets :

> " There's a light about to break,
> There's a day about to dawn :
> Men of thought, and men of action !
>   Clear the way ! "

Consider, next, the influence of the spirit of Poetry as distinguished from the particular form in which it may be manifested.

The poets of the higher order are susceptible of a still further subdivision.   There are those who project themselves out of their own particular being, and become by imagination one with that on which they meditate : and those who inform all they gaze on with their own individuality.   Those, that is, who sympathise with all that is created : and those whose imagination makes all to sympathise with them.   I need not say which of these two classes is the

domain of the higher Poetry.   Wherever egoism
enters, whether it be into life or into art, it
degrades and narrows ; he through whom the
universe speaks what God intended it to speak,
is, as a poet, greater than he who through all
the universe still only speaks out himself.

Now remark the different influence of these
classes.

First, we have those whose imagination represents all nature as sympathising with them ;
and just as through a coloured glass a landscape
looks red, blue, or yellow, as the glass may be
tinted, so does one feeling modify all others,
and colour all things with its own hue.   In
some measure this is true of us all.

> " I may not hope from outward forms to win
> The passion and the life, whose fountains are within.
> O Lady ! we receive but what we give,
> And in our life alone does nature live :
> Ours is her wedding garment, ours her shroud ! " *

We all possess this tendency when the
imagination has been intensified by one single
passion or narrowed by one absorbing pursuit.
Let me give you a very homely illustration.   I
was once passing through the finest street in England on the outside of a mail coach.   A young
woman who sat near me, when we had reached
the end of the street, suddenly exclaimed, " I
never saw so many narrow doors in all my life ! "

* Coleridge—" Ode to Dejection."

When the first surprise, produced by an exclamation so much in discord with my own thoughts, had subsided, I began to make inquiries, and discovered that her father was a builder. The builder's daughter had cast the hue of her daily associations over everything. To her the buildings grey with the hoar of ages were as if they were not: historical interest, architectural beauty, solemn associations did not exist. To her there was nothing there but stones, graven by the stonemason's chisel, and doors, measurable by the rule of the carpenter. And in the same way do we all colour nature with our own pursuits. To a sportsman, a rich field is covert for game : to a farmer, the result of guano : to a geologist, indication of a certain character of subjacent rock.

It is very instructive to observe how superstition can thus summon all nature to be the minister of our human history, especially when it is rendered more imperious in its demands by pride. There is scarcely an ancient family which has not the tradition of preternatural appearances preceding the death or connected with the destinies of the chief members of the race. Shakspere, as usual, gives us this. Lear's anguish sheds the hue of ingratitude over the heavens. To Timon, sun, and moon, and stars are tinctured with his misanthropy. To Macbeth, meditating murder, all nature is preternatural, sounds of simple instinct ominous, and all things conscious of his secret.

> " Now o'er the one half-world
> Nature seems dead, and wicked dreams abuse
> The curtain'd sleep ; now witchcraft celebrates
> Pale Hecate's offerings ; and withered murther,
> Alarum'd by his sentinel, the wolf,
> Whose howl 's his watch, thus with his stealthy pace,
> With Tarquin's ravishing strides, towards his design
> Moves like a ghost.   Thou sure and firm-set earth,
> Hear not my steps, which way they walk, for fear
> Thy very stone prate of my whereabout,
> And take the present horror from the time,
> Which now suits with it."

> " Come sealing night,
> Scarf up the tender eye of pitiful day ;
> And, with thy bloody and invisible hand,
> Cancel, and tear to pieces, that great bond
> Which keeps me pale !   Light thickens ; and the crow
> Makes wing to the rooky wood ;
> Good things of day begin to droop and drowse ;
> While night's black agents to their prey do rouse !"

Observe, again, how Casca's conscience already half-burdened, distorts the simplest phenomena :—

> " Against the capitol I met a lion,
> Who glared upon me, and went surly by
> Without annoying me ; and there were drawn
> Upon a heap a hundred ghastly women
> Transformed with their fear ; who swore they saw
> Men all in fire walk up and down the streets.
> And yesterday, the bird of night did sit
> Even at noonday, upon the market place,
> Hooting and shrieking."

Of all this apparent supernaturalism, Cicero gives the true account, in reply :—

> "Indeed, it is a strange disposed time ;
> But men may construe things after their fashion,
> Clean from the purpose of the things themselves."

And Calphurnia, with a presentiment of her husband's doom :—

> "There is one within,
> Besides the things that we have heard and seen,
> Recounts most horrid sights seen by the watch.
> A lioness hath whelped in the streets :
> And graves have yawned and yielded up their dead :
> Fierce, fiery warriors fight upon the clouds,
> In ranks and squadrons and right form of war,
> Which drizzled blood upon the capitol :
> The noise of battle hurtled in the air,
> Horses do neigh, and dying men did groan :
> And ghosts did shriek and squeal about the streets."

Mark, too, how, as I said, pride has its share in giving shape to this superstition. Cæsar replies, the valour of the conqueror defying omens, and the large heart of the man recognising his sub-jection to the laws of a common humanity :

> "Yet Cæsar shall go forth : for these predictions
> Are to the world in general, as to Cæsar."

But Calphurnia, with that worship of high birth which is peculiar to the feminine nature, answers :—

> "When beggars die there are no comets seen :
> The heavens themselves blaze forth the death of princes."

So wonderful is that egoism of man which can thus overspread the heavens with its woes, and read in the planets only prophecies of himself! Now that which belongs to us all in some moods is characteristic of some poets through all their nature, and pervades their work. The influence, therefore, of this class of Poetry, depends upon the *man*. The self which is thrown upon nature may be the lower or the higher self, and the influence will be correspondingly of the lower or the higher kind.

Among the former divisions of the egoistic class of first-rate poets, severe justice compels me with pain to place Lord Byron. Brought up under the baleful influences of Calvinism, which makes sovereign Will the measure of Right, instead of Right the cause and law of Will, a system which he all his life hated and believed — fancying himself the mark of an inexorable decree, and bidding a terrible defiance to the unjust One who had fixed his doom—no wonder that, as in that strange phenomenon the spectre of the Brocken, the traveller sees a gigantic form cast upon the mists, which he discovers at last to be but his own shadow ; so, the noble poet went through life haunted, turn which way he would, with the gigantic shadow of himself, which obscured the heavens and turned the light into thick darkness.

Foremost among those in whom a higher self

informs all objects, stands Milton. We are compelled to place him with those in whom egoism is not wholly absorbed in nature. Shakspere is a "voice." Read Shakspere through, and, except from some of his sonnets, you could not guess who or what manner of man he was. But you could not read Milton long without discovering the man through the poet. His domestic miseries are reflected in his Samson Agonistes. In his Comus, that majestic psalm to Chastity, are blended the antique heroism of his Pagan studies, and the Christian sanctities of his rare manhood. His very angels reason upon Puritan questions; and it was the taunt of Pope, that in the Eternal lips themselves, redemption is a contrivance or scheme according to the systematic theology of a school divine. And yet the egoism with which all his Poetry is impregnated is the egoism of a glorious nature. If we were asked who in the eighteen Christian centuries stands before us as the highest approximation to what we conceive as Christian manhood, in which are rarely blended the opposites of purity and passion, gracefulness and strength, sanctity and manifold fitness for all the worldly duties of the man and the citizen, we should scarcely hesitate to answer—John Milton. The poet is overshadowed by the individual man : but the influence of the man is all for good.

Now compare with these the poets who see in Nature not themselves, but Nature; who are her voice, not she theirs. Of this class, likewise, there are two divisions : the first represented by Shakspere, the second by Wordsworth.

Shakspere is an universal poet, because he utters all that is in men; Wordsworth, because he speaks that which is in all men. There is much difference between these two statements.

The perfection of Shakspere, like all the highest perfection, consists, not in the predominance of a single quality, or feeling, but in the just balance and perfect harmony of all. You cannot say whether the tragic element of our nature, or the comic, predominates; whether he has more sympathy with its broad laugh, or its secret sigh; with the contemplativeness of Hamlet, which lets the moment of action pass, or the promptitude of Hotspur; with the aristocratic pride of Coriolanus, which cannot deign to canvass the mob for votes, or the coarse wit and human instincts of the serving men.

Wordsworth, on the contrary, gives to us humanity stripped of its peculiarities; the feelings which do not belong to this man or that, this or that age, but are the heritage of our common nature. "That," says he in a private letter, "which will distinguish my poems hereafter from those of other poets, is this : that while other poets laboured to exhibit that which distinguishes one man from another, especially the dramatic poets, I have made it my concern to exhibit that which is common to all men."

As a specimen of this, take that well-known poem :

" She was a Phantom of delight,
    When first she gleamed upon my sight :
    A lovely Apparition, sent
    To be a moment's ornament ;
    Her eyes as stars of Twilight fair ;
    Like Twilight's, too, her dusky hair ;
    But all things else about her drawn
    From May-time's brightest, loveliest dawn ;
    A dancing shape, an image gay,
    To haunt, to startle, and way-lay.

" I saw her upon nearer view,
    A Spirit, yet a Woman too !
    Her household motions light and free,
    And steps of virgin liberty ;
    A countenance in which did meet
    Sweet records, promises as sweet ;
    A Creature not too bright or good
    For human nature's daily food ;
    For transient sorrows, simple wiles,
    Praise, blame, love, kisses, tears, and smiles.

" And now I see with eye serene
    The very pulse of the machine ;
    A Being breathing thoughtful breath,
    A Traveller between life and death ;
    The reason firm, the temperate will,
    Endurance, foresight, strength, and skill ;

A perfect Woman, nobly planned,
To warn, to comfort, and command ;
And yet a Spirit still, and bright,
With something of an angel light."

You will observe that it is not a portrait like
one of Shakspere's, in which, gradually, a particular female character unfolds a personality
which belongs to Miranda or to Juliet, and
could not belong to Cleopatra or to Lady
Macbeth: nor a description like Tennyson's,
which, if true of Isabel or Lilian, must be
false of Adeline or Eleanore: nor, again, this
or that woman, coloured in the false hues
which passion or fancy have thrown on her for
a time: but womanhood in its essence, and
divested of its peculiarities of nation or century :
such as her Creator meant her to be: such as
every woman is potentially if not actually :
such as she appears successively to the lover,
the husband, and the friend, separating from
such lover, husband, and friend, the accidents
of an English, Spanish, or French temperament.
And yet, remark that this womanhood, so
painted, is not a mere thin, unsubstantial
abstraction of the intellect; but a living,
tangible image, appreciable by the senses, a
single, total impression, "sensuous," as Milton
says of Poetry: else it would not be Poetry,
but a scientific definition. You have before
you an ideal clothed in flesh and blood,

without the limitations of any particular idiosyncrasy.

This is the sense in which poets like Wordsworth are universal poets and free from egoism ; very different from the sense in which Shakspere is universal.

Now to compare the various influences of these poets. And, first, to compare class with class. The poet in whom individuality predominates will have a more definite influence : he of whom universality is the characteristic, a more wide and lasting one. The influence of Cowper, Milton, or Byron, on individuals is distinct and appreciable : that of Homer and Shakspere, almost imperceptible on single minds, is spread silently over ages, and determines the character of the world's literature and the world's feeling.

Comparing each class with itself, and taking first that which we have characterized as the more egoistic, the more popular will be almost always the less pure, because the passionate enthusiasm for what is great and good is shared by few, comparatively with the power of comprehending the might and force of what we commonly call the passions. Milton is placed with honour on our shelves. We read Byron through and through.

Next, of the poets of nature, Shakspere, and the very few who can be ranked with him, will be more popular than such as Wordsworth ; not because he is greater, though he is, of course, immeasurably, but because his greatness, like that of nature's self, is broken into fragments, and all can find in him something corresponding with their humour. Only a few, like Herschel and Humboldt, can comprehend with something like adequateness the Cosmos, or Order of the Universe ; there is no one who cannot read a page of it. And so, very few of those who talk of Shakspere's greatness, know *how* great he is ; but all can mark with pencil dashes certain lines and detached acts ; and if you examined the copy so dashed and marked, you would probably discover what in Shakspere bears, or was supposed to bear, reference to the reader's own character, or more properly, illustrated his or her private prejudices, peculiarities, and personal history ; but, unless a hand as free from egoism as Shakspere's own had drawn the lines of approval, you would gain from the book of extracts made up of all such passages, not the nature of Man, but the idiosyncrasy of a man. Tell us, therefore, that a man's favourite poet is such as Wordsworth, and we know something about his character ; but tell us that he delights in Shakspere, and we know as yet no more of him than if it had been said that life has joys for him. He may be a Marlborough, or he may be a clown.

Permit me to offer you two pieces of advice, resulting from what has been said.

First, Cultivate universality of taste. There is no surer mark of a half-educated mind than the incapacity of admiring various forms of excellence. Men who cannot praise Dryden without dispraising Coleridge; nor feel the stern, earthly truthfulness of Crabbe without disparaging the wild, ethereal, impalpable music of Shelley; nor exalt Spenser except by sneering at Tennyson, are precisely the persons to whom it should in consistency seem strange that in God's world there is a place for the eagle and the wren, a separate grace to the swan and the humming-bird, their own fragrance to the cedar and the violet. Enlarge your tastes, that you may enlarge your hearts as well as your pleasures : feel all that is beautiful— love all that is good. The first maxim in religion and in art is—sever yourself from all sectarianism ; pledge yourself to no school ; cut your life adrift from all party; be a slave to no maxims ; stand forth, unfettered and free, servant only to the truth. And if you say, " But this will force each of us to stand alone": I reply—Yes, grandly alone! untrammelled by the prejudices of any, and free to admire the beauty, and love the goodness of them all.

Secondly, of the writers whom we called egoistic, in whom, that is, the man predominates over the poet, choose such only as are the un-feigned servants of goodness—I do not mean *goodliness*—to be your special favourites. In early life, it is, I believe, from this class solely that our favourites are selected : and a man's character and mind are moulded for good or evil far more by the forms of imagination which surround his childhood than by any subsequent scientific training. We can recollect how a couplet from the frontispiece of a hymn-book struck deeper roots into our being, and has borne more manifest fruits, than all the formal training we ever got. Or we can trace, as unerringly as an Indian on the trail, the several influences of each poet through our lives : the sense of unjust destiny which was created by Byron ; the taint of Moore's voluptuousness ; the hearty, healthful life of Scott ; the calming power of Wordsworth ; the masculine vigour of Dryden. For it is only in after years that the real taste for the very highest Poetry is acquired. Life, and experience, as well as mental cultiva-tion, are indispensable. In earlier life the influence of the man is mightier than that of the poet. Therefore, let every young man especially guard his heart and imagination against the mastery of those writers who sap his vigour and taint his purity.

We proceed to name a few of the modes in which Poetry does actually influence men :

First.   In the way of giving relief to feeling. It is a law of our nature that strong feeling, unexpressed either in words or action, becomes morbid. You need not dread the passionate man, whose wrath vents itself in words : dread the man who grows pale, and suppresses the language of his resentment.   There is something in him yet to come out.   This is the secret of England's freedom from revolution and conspiracies : she has free discussion.   Wrongs do not smoulder silently, to burst forth un-expectedly.   Every grievance may have a hear-ing, and not being pent up, spends itself before it is dangerous.

> " The land where, girt by friend or foe,
>   A man may speak the thing he will." *

Now, there are feelings which, unuttered, would make a man dangerous—or morbid—or mad ;—utterance relieves, and, weakening the *feeling*, makes the *man* strong.

> " To me alone there came a thought of grief :
>   A timely utterance gave that thought relief,
>   And I again am strong."

For such feelings the poets find us suitable expression.   In an artificial state of society, perhaps some young, warlike spirit pines for a more dangerous life than our quiet days give. Well, he reads Scott's border raids, or " Scots wha hae wi' Wallace bled," or Hohen Linden,

* Tennyson.

and the vivid forms of imagination receive, as it were, his superfluous energies, and the chafing subsides in unreal battle-fields : or some diseased germ of misanthropy is enlarging in his heart—secret discontent with life ; disagreement with the world; conflict between his nature and civil regulations. Let him read Byron—a dangerous cure—but in the end a certain one. Byron has said all that can be said upon the subject. What more can be added ? There is no restless feeling left behind of something unsaid. Exhaustion follows—then health. For it is a mistake to think that Poetry is only good to nurse feeling. It is good for enabling us to *get rid* of feeling for which there is no available field of action. It is the safety-valve to the heart.

It has, besides, an elevating influence. It breaks the monotonous flatness of existence by excitement. Its very essence is that it exalts us, and puts us in a higher mood than that in which we live habitually. And this is peculiarly true of modern Poetry. A great critic * has said that the distinction between ancient and modern Poetry is, that the characteristic of the former is satisfaction, that of the latter aspiration. To the ancients this time-world was all. To round it with completeness, and hold all powers in harmonious balance, was their whole aim. Whereas,

* Schlegel.

Christianity has dwarfed this life in comparison with the thought of an endless existence which it has revealed. To them the thought of death only came as a stimulus to increased enjoyment of that which must soon pass. To us that thought comes moderating and calming all pleasure. And hence the sad, dark character of Christian, especially northern Poetry ; as the utterance of a heart which is conscious of eternal discord rather than of perfection of powers ; and through it all there vibrates an under-tone of melancholy, adding even to mirth a peculiar pathos. Is it not better that it should be so ? Does not such poetry therefore more peculiarly belong to Working Men, whose life is desire, not enjoyment ; aspiration, not contentment ?

Whoever will go into any Gothic cathedral in the evening, knowing nothing of the connoisseurship of architecture, and watch the effect produced on his mind by the lines which wander away, bewildering the eye with the feeling of endlessness, and losing themselves in the dark distances, and will then compare the total impression with that produced by the voluptuous, earthly beauty of a temple like the Madeleine in Paris, will understand, without the help of any scientific jargon, the difference between the ancient idea of satisfaction and the modern one of aspiration.

But when we say that Poetry elevates, let it not be understood of the improvement of physical comforts. Poetry will not place a man in better circumstances ; but it may raise him above his circumstances, and fortify him with inward independence ; as Lovelace, the cavalier poet, has very gracefully expressed, in lines written in confinement :—

> " Stone walls do not a prison make,
>   Nor iron bars a cage ;
>   Minds innocent and quiet take
>   That for a hermitage.

> " If I have freedom in my love,
>   And in my soul am free,
>   Angels alone, that soar above,
>   Enjoy such liberty."

And yet, as there are some persons who cannot conceive of human elevation except as connected with circumstantial condition, I must tell you an anecdote to satisfy even them. A lady, with whose friendship I am honoured, was travelling last summer in the Lake district of Cumberland and Westmoreland. Being interested in education, she visited many of the National Schools in that country. For the most part the result was uninteresting enough. The heavy looks and stolid intellects, which characterise our English agricultural population, disappointed her. But in one place there was a striking difference. The children were sprightly, alert, and answered with intelligence all the questions proposed; traced rivers from their sources to the sea, explaining why the towns along their course were of such and such a character, and how the soil had modified the habits and lives of the inhabitants—with much of similar information. The schoolmaster had been educated at one of our great training seminaries. He was invited by the tourist to spend an hour at the hotel; and when, after a long conversation, she expressed her surprise that one so highly educated should bury himself in a retired, unknown spot, with small stipend, teaching only a few rustics, he replied, after some hesitation—" Why, Madam, when this situation was first offered me, I was on the point of marriage; and I calculated that it would be worth more to me to live on a small salary, with domestic peace, in the midst of this beautiful scenery, than on a much larger sum in a less glorious spot."

Now, there are people who can only estimate the worth of a thing by what it will bring. What is the *use* of Poetry? Well, perhaps they may answer that question for themselves, if I have shown that refined taste may be an equivalent for half an income, and a sense of what is beautiful in God's world may make a poor man

" passing rich with forty pounds a-year."

The tendency, again, of Poetry is to unite men together. And this both indirectly and directly.

It has been already said that the highest Poetry is that which represents the most universal feeling, not the most rare. It is in this sense that Milton's definition makes Poetry " simple "; that is, it deals with the feelings which we have in common, as men, and not with those which we possess as a particular sort or class of men ; with the natural rather than the trained, artificial, or acquired feelings ; just as the botanist is simple in contrast with the horticulturist. The one seeks what is natural ; and to him nothing in nature is a weed. The other seeks rarities and hot-bed monstrosities.

The Germans say that the world has produced only three poets of first-rate genius : Homer, Shakspere, and Goëthe. This, I suppose, is an exaggeration : nevertheless, it is true that the highest poets have been, like them, not a class or caste, but of humanity. Take, almost at a venture, the first familiar names that present themselves.

Milton, by all the associations of education and refined taste, belonged to the royalists and the church ; but he threw himself, in spite of the vulgarities which repelled him personally from its worship and left him at last without visible worship, on the side of the conventicle, because in the days of the Stuarts the cause of the conventicle was the cause of liberty and truth.

Dante was a Romanist ; but no slave was he of popery. His world-wide conception represents the heathens and the Christians of all ages as the subjects of one moral government, responsible to the laws impressed upon humanity rather than those written by the Church ; and his severe justice does not scruple to consign a long list of bishops and popes to the eternal penalty of crimes.

Or, again, Byron and Shelley—aristocrats both by birth, yet no minions of a caste, nor champions of hereditary privilege—they were men ; and their power lay in this, that they were the champions of human rights, as well as utterers of the passion that is in men. So far as they are great, they are universal ; so far as they are small or bad, they are narrow and egotistical. And as time rolls on, that which is of self, limited and evil, will become obsolete, and wither, as the mortal warp and woof shrivelled on the arm of Halbert Glendinning, when he plunged it into the sacred flame to grasp the Volume of Truth at the bidding of the White Lady of Avenel ; and that of their works which will remain unconsumed will be the living flesh of the humanity that never dies —so much as is true to universal nature and to fact.

It is thus that the poets universalise and unite. " One touch of nature makes the whole world kin." And, hence, Poetry has been silently doing a work for the poorer classes when they were not aware of it ; for even that Poetry which does not interest them, may be opening the hearts of the richer classes towards them. Did Burns teach the nobles no sympathy with the cares, and the loves, and the trials of the cotter's life ? And when poor Hood wrote the " Song of the Shirt," so touchingly expressive of the sorrows of an unknown class, the over-worked needlewoman, and all England thrilled to the appeal :

> " O men, with sisters dear !
> O men with mothers and wives !
> It is not linen you're wearing out,
> But human creatures' lives "—

and when, in consequence, plan after plan was tried, and investigations instituted, and a kindlier interest evoked to ameliorate their condition, tell us—Had Poetry done nothing for the Working Classes ?

But it has a more direct influence than this in the way of uniting. Chiefly from that power with which the poetic nature is peculiarly gifted of discovering what Shakspere calls the "soul of goodness in things evil." Every great poet is a " double natured man " ; with the feminine and manly powers in harmonious union ; having the tact, and the sympathy, and the intuition, and the tenderness of woman, with the breadth and massiveness of the manly intellect, besides the calm justice which is almost exclusively masculine. For this reason a poet, seeing into the life of things, is not one-sided ; can see the truth which lies at the root of error ; can blame evil without hysterically raving against every doer of it ; distinguishes between frailty and villainy ; judges leniently, because by sympathy, he can look upon faults as they appear to those who committed them ; judges justly, because so far as he is an artist, he can regard the feeling with which he sympathises from without ; in a double way—realising it, but not surrendered to it.

I must quote two passages explanatory of the world of meaning contained in those few words of Shakspere : the " soul of goodness in things evil."

Wordsworth means the same when he says :—

" 'Tis Nature's law
    That none, the meanest of created things,
    Of forms created the most vile and brute,
    The dullest or most noxious, should exist,
    Divorced from good—a spirit and pulse of good,
    A life and soul, to every mode of being
    Inseparably linked.   Then be assured
    That least of all can aught—that ever owned
    The heaven-regarding eye and front sublime
    Which man is born to, sink, howe'er depressed,

> So low as to be scorned without a sin ;
> Without offence to God cast out of view."

And again :—

> " He who feels contempt
> For any living thing, hath faculties
> That he hath never used : and Thought with him
> Is in its infancy :"

One of the best illustrations I can remember of this prerogative of the poet to fasten the attention on what is human and lovable, rather than on what is evil, is Hood's " Bridge of Sighs." This little poem is suggested by the sight of a poor suicide, who has cast herself from one of the London bridges. Prudery, male or female, would turn from such a spectacle with disgust : the disciple of some school of cold divinity would see in it only a text for a discourse on hell. The poet discerns something in it of a deeper mystery, not so flippantly to be solved. He bids you

> " Touch her not scornfully,
> Think of her mournfully,
> Gently and humanly ;
> Not of the stains of her ;
> All that remains of her
> Now is pure womanly.
> Make no deep scrutiny
> Into her mutiny
> Rash and undutiful,
> Past all dishonour,
> Death has left on her
> Only the beautiful."

And observe how, with exquisite truthfulness, he fixes your attention, not upon that in which the poor outcast differs from you, but on that in which her sisterhood to the human family consisted—and, for aught *you* may dare to say, still consists—

> "Wonderment guesses
> Where was her home?
> Who was her father?
> Who was her mother?
> Had she a sister?
> Had she a brother?
> Or was there a nearer one
> Still, and a dearer one
> Yet, than all other?"

And mark how—without any feeble sentimentalism, without once confusing the boundaries of right and wrong, without hinting a suspicion that vice is not vice, and wrong not wrong—he simply reminds you that judgment does not belong to you, a fellow-creature and a sinner; and bids you place her in the attitude in which alone *you* have a right to regard her now—

> "Cross her hands humbly,
> As if praying dumbly,
> Over her breast;
> Owning her weakness,
> Her evil behaviour,
> And leaving in meekness
> Her sins to her Saviour."

I should not like to be the woman who could

read that poem without something more than sentimental tears, an enlarged humanity, and a deeper justice; nor should I like to be the man who could rise from the perusal of it without a mighty throb added to the conviction that libertinism is a thing of damnable and selfish cowardice.

Again, Poetry discovers good in men who differ from us, and so teaches us that we are one with them. For the poet belongs to the world rather than to his party: speaks his party's feelings, which are human: not their watchwords and formulas, which, being forms of the intellect, are transitory, often false, always limited. Thus, Romanism and Puritanism, and their modern feeble descendants, as dogmatic systems, are forbidding enough. But listen to Dante, and you will feel that purgatory, false as a dogma, is true as the symbolism of an everlasting fact of the human soul. Hear Milton sing, and the *heart* of Puritanism is recognised as a noble and a manly thing. And, however repelled you may be by the false metaphysics, the pretensions to infallible interpretations, the cant phrases, and the impotent intolerance which characterize the dwarfed and dwindled Puritanism of our own days, out of which all pith and manhood appear to have departed, who does not feel disposed to be tender to it for Cowper's gentle sake? However out of date the effort of the Tractarian may seem to you, to reproduce the piety of the past through the forms of the past, instead of striving, like a true prophet, to interpret the aspirations of the present in forms which shall truly represent and foster them, what man is there to whose heart Keble has not shown that in Tractarianism, too, there is a "soul of goodness," a life and a meaning which mere negations cannot destroy ?

Lastly, I name the refining influence of Poetry. We shall confine our proofs to that which it has already done in making men and life less savage, carnal, and mercenary ; and this especially in the three departments which were the peculiar sphere of the Poetry which is called romantic. Beneath its influence, passion became love ; selfishness, honour ; and war, chivalry.

The first of these, as a high sentiment, can only be said to have come into existence with the Christianity of the Middle Ages. All who are familiar with the Greek and Roman Poetry, know that the sentiment which now bears the name, was unknown to the ancients. It became what it is when passion had been hallowed by imagination. Then, and not till then, it became loyalty to female worth, consecrated by religion. For the sacred thought of a Virgin Mother spread its sanctity over the whole idea of the sex. Christianity had given to the world a

new object for its imagination ; and the idolatry
into which it passed in the Church of Rome,
was but the inevitable result of the effort of
rude minds struggling to express in form the
new idea of a divine sacredness belonging to
feminine qualities of meekness and purity,
which the ages before had overlooked. That
this influence of the religious element of the
imagination on the earthlier feeling is not
fanciful but historical, might be shown in the
single case of Ignatius Loyola, on whose ardent
temperament the influences of his age worked
strongly. Hence it was that there seemed
nothing profane when the chivalrous gallantry
of the soldier transformed itself by, to him, a
most natural transition, into a loyal dedication
of all his powers to One who was "not a
countess, nor a duchess, but much greater."
But only think how he must have shrunk from
this transference of homage, as blasphemous, if
his former earthlier feelings had not been
elevated by a religious imagination ; if, in short,
his affections had been like those of the Greeks
and Romans!

And while on the subject of the influence of
all the higher feelings in elevating passion into
that which is unselfish and pure, and even
sublime, I will remind you of those glorious
lines of Lovelace in reply to a reproach on
account of absence caused by duty :

"Yet this inconstancy is such
　　As you, too, shall adore ;
　I could not love thee, dear, so much,
　　Loved I not honour more."

Under the influence of imagination, selfishness became honour. Doubtless, the law of
honour is only half Christian. Yet it did this :
it proclaimed the invisible truth above the
visible comfort. It consecrated certain acts as
right, uncalculatingly, and independently of
consequences. It did not say—it will be *better*
for you in the end if you do honourably. It
said—you *must* do honourably, though it be not
better for you to do it, but worse, and deathful.
It was not religion ; but it was better than the
popular, merely prudential, mercenary religion,
which says, " Honesty is the best policy : godli-
ness is gain : do right and you will not lose by
it." Honour said, Perhaps you *will* lose—all—
life : lose then, like a man ; for there is something higher than life, dearer than even *your*
eternal gain. It was not purely religious : for
it retained the selfish element. But it was a
more refined selfishness which permitted a man
to take another's life in defence of his honour,
than that which requires him to do it in defence
of his purse.

Finally, through poetic imagination war became chivalry. The practice of arms ceased to
be " a conflict of kites and crows " ; it was

guarded by a refined courtesy from every rude
and ungenerous abuse of superior strength.

Upon this point there is much sophistry
prevalent ; therefore it is worth while to see how
the matter really stands.   A truly great man—
the American Channing—has said, I remember,
somewhere in his works, that if armies were
dressed in a hangman's or a butcher's garb, the
false glare of military enthusiasm would be
destroyed, and war would be seen in its true
aspect as butchery.

It is wonderful how the generous enthusiasm
of Dr Channing has led him into such a sophism.
Take away honour, and imagination and Poetry
from war, and it becomes carnage.   Doubtless.
And take away public spirit and invisible principles from resistance to a tax, and Hampden
becomes a noisy demagogue.   Take away the
grandeur of his cause, and Washington is a
rebel, instead of the purest of patriots.   Take
away imagination from love, and what remains ?
Let a people treat with scorn the defenders of
its liberties, and invest them with the symbols
of degradation, and it will soon have no one to
defend it.   This is but a truism.

But it is a falsity if it implies that the mere
change of symbolic dress, unless the dress truly
represented a previous change of public feeling,
would reverse the feeling with which the profession of arms is regarded.   So long as people

found it impossible to confound the warrior
with the hangman, all that a change of garb
could do would be to invest the sign with
new dignity. Things mean become noble by
association : the Thistle—the Leek—the Broom
of the Plantagenets—the Garter—and the
Death's Head and Cross Bones on the front
of the Black Brunswickers, typical of the stern
resolve to avenge their Chief—methinks those
symbols did not exactly change the soldier into
a sexton !

But the truth is that here, as elsewhere, Poetry
has reached the truth, while science and
common-sense have missed it. It has distinguished—as, in spite of all mercenary and feeble
sophistry, men ever will distinguish—war from
mere bloodshed. It has discerned the higher
feelings which lie beneath its revolting features.
Carnage is terrible. The conversion of pro-
ducers into destroyers is a calamity. Death,
and insults to woman worse than death—and
human features obliterated beneath the hoof
of the war-horse—and reeking hospitals, and
ruined commerce, and violated homes, and
broken hearts—they are all awful. But there
is something worse than death. Cowardice is
worse. And the decay of enthusiasm and
manliness is worse. And it is worse than death,
aye, worse than a hundred thousand deaths,
when a people has gravitated down into the

creed that the " wealth of nations " consists, not in generous hearts—" Fire in each breast, and freedom on each brow "—in national virtues, and primitive simplicity, and heroic endurance, and preference of duty to life ;—not in MEN, but in silk, and cotton, and something that they call " capital." Peace is blessed. Peace, arising out of charity. But peace, springing out of the calculations of selfishness, is not blessed. If the price to be paid for peace is this, that wealth accumulate and men decay, better far that every street in every town of our once noble country should run blood !

Through the physical horrors of warfare, Poetry discerned the redeeming nobleness. For in truth, when war is not prolonged, the kindling of all the higher passions prevents the access of the baser ones. A nation split and severed by mean religious and political dissensions, suddenly feels its unity and men's hearts beat together, at the mere possibility of invasion. And even woman, as the author of the " History of the Peninsular War " has well remarked, sufferer as she is by war, yet gains ; in the more chivalrous respect paid to her, in the elevation of the feelings excited towards her, in the attitude of protection assumed by men, and in the high calls to duty which arouse her from the frivolousness and feebleness into which her existence is apt to sink.

I will illustrate this by one more anecdote from the same campaign to which allusion has already been made—Sir Charles Napier's campaign against the robber tribes of Upper Scinde.

A detachment of troops was marching along a valley, the cliffs overhanging which were crested by the enemy. A sergeant, with eleven men, chanced to become separated from the rest by taking the wrong side of a ravine, which they expected soon to terminate, but which suddenly deepened into an impassable chasm. The officer in command signalled to the party an order to return. They mistook the signal for a command to charge ; the brave fellows answered with a cheer, and charged. At the summit of the steep mountain was a triangular platform, defended by a breastwork, behind which were seventy of the foe. On they went, charging up one of those fearful paths, eleven against seventy. The contest could not long be doubtful with such odds. One after another they fell : six upon the spot, the remainder hurled backwards ; but not until they had slain nearly twice their own number.

There is a custom, we are told, amongst the hillsmen, that when a great chieftain of their own falls in battle, his wrist is bound with a thread either of red or green, the red denoting the highest rank. According to custom, they stripped the dead, and threw their bodies over the precipice.   When their comrades came, they found their corpses stark and gashed; but round both wrists of every British hero was twined the red thread ! *

I think you will perceive how Poetry, expressing in this rude symbolism unutterable admiration of heroic daring, had given another aspect to war than that of butchery: and you will understand how, with such a foe, and such a general as the English commander, who more than once refused battle because the wives and children of the enemy were in the hostile camp, and he feared for their lives, carnage changed its character, and became chivalry: and how it was that the British troops learned to treat their captive women with respect: and the chieftains of the Cutchee hills offered their swords and services with enthusiasm to their conqueror ; and the wild hill-tribes, transplanted to the plains, became as persevering in agriculture as they had been before in war.

And now to conclude.   They tell us that scenes such as this may be called for in this our England.   I do not pretend to judge.   We only know that a military nation is at our doors with 450,000 gallant soldiers under arms, every man burning to wipe out the memory of past defeats, with one at their head the prestige of

* " History of the Administration of Scinde," by Lieut.-Gen. Sir William Napier.

whose name recalls an era of unparalleled brilliancy, many of them trained in a school of warfare where the razzias of Africa have not taught either scrupulosity or mercifulness. We know that a chieftain who is to rule France with any hope of imperial influence, can best secure enthusiasm by giving victory to her armies; and that French generals have already specified the way in which—I quote the words of Paixhan—a lesson might be taught to England which she should not soon forget.

No one who loves his country,—no one who knows what is meant by the *sack of a town,* especially by French soldiers—can contemplate the possibility of such an event, without a fervent hope that that day may never come. Nor does it become us to boast ; the enthusiasm of the platform is easy, and costs little: and we may be called upon, before very long, to show by something more than words, whether there be steel in our hearts and hands, or not.

But thus much I will dare to say. If a foreign foot be planted on our sacred soil—if the ring of the rifle of the Chasseurs de Vincennes be heard upon these shores, terrible as the first reverses might be, when discipline could be met only by raw enthusiasm—thanks to gentlemen who have taught us the sublime mysteries of " capital " in lieu of the old English superstitions of Honour and Religion—they may yet chance to learn that British Chivalry did not breathe her last at Moodkee or Ferozeshah, or Sobraon, or Goojerat, or Meeanee, or Hyderabad. They may yet be taught that there is something beyond the raw hysterics of a transient excitement in the spirit of self-sacrifice which we have learned from our Master's cross. They may yet discover that amongst the artizans, and peasants, and working men of England, there are a thousand thousand worthy to be brothers of those heroic eleven who sleep beneath the rocks of Trukkee, with the red thread of Honour round their wrists.

WORDSWORTH

A Lecture delivered to the Members of the Brighton Athenæum, on February 10th, 1853

IN order to treat fully the subject which I have to bring before you this evening, I believe there are three points to which I ought principally to direct your attention. The first is, the qualifications necessary for appreciating poetry in general, and for appreciating the poetry of Wordsworth in particular. The second is the character and life of Wordsworth, so far as they bear upon his poetry, and so far as they may have been supposed to have formed or modified his peculiar poetical theories and principles. The third point is, the theories and poetical principles of Wordsworth, and how far they are true, how far they have been exaggerated, and how far Wordsworth has himself worked out the principles he has laid down.

Now, it will be plain that the last of these is the most important point of all: it is, in fact, *the* subject of our consideration; but so many preliminary subjects have presented themselves which must be gone into before we enter upon this, that I have found it necessary to reserve this third topic for a succeeding lecture,* confining myself on the present occasion merely to the first two points that I have already named.

I have undertaken to lecture this evening upon Wordsworth. To some persons this will appear presumption; to others, it will appear superfluous. To all the admirers of Wordsworth's genius, it will appear presumption. To these I simply reply, I know well the difficulty of the subject, I know how impossible it is to treat it adequately; I am aware that presumption is implied in the thought, that before it is possible to criticise a man one must sympathise with him, and that to sympathise with a man implies that there is, to a certain extent, a power of breathing the same atmosphere. Nevertheless, I reply that it is with me, at least, a work and labour of love; nor can I believe, that any one who has for years studied Wordsworth and loved him, and year by year felt his appreciation and comprehension of Wordsworth grow, and has during all those years endeavoured to make Wordsworth's principles the guiding principles of his own inner life—I cannot believe that such a man can have nothing to

* This lecture was never delivered, owing to Mr Robertson's ill-health.

say which it is desirable should be heard by his fellow men.

There is another class, however, to whom such a subject will seem superfluous; for the general opinion about Wordsworth is exceedingly superficial. To the mass of the public all that is known of Wordsworth is a conception something like this : They have heard of an old man who lived somewhere in the Lake districts, who raved considerably of Lake scenery, who wrote a large number of small poems, all of them innocent, many of them puerile and much laughed at, at the time they appeared, by clever men; that they were lashed in the reviews, and annihilated by Lord Byron, as, for instance, in those well-known lines—

"A drowsy, frowsy poem, called the Excursion,
    Writ in a manner which is my aversion ;"

and that he was guilty of a vast mass of other verses, all exceedingly innocent, and at the same time exceedingly dull and heavy. It is this class of persons whom I ask on the present occasion to listen quietly to the first subject I have to bring before them—the qualifications necessary for appreciating poetry in general and Wordsworth's poetry in particular.

Now, the first qualification I shall speak of as necessary for appreciating poetry is unworldliness. Let us understand the term employed. By worldliness, I mean entanglement in the tem-

poral and visible.   It is the spirit of worldliness
which makes a man love show, splendour, rank,
title, and sensual enjoyments; and occupies his
attention, chiefly or entirely, with conversations
respecting merely passing events, and passing
acquaintances.   I know not that I could give a
more distinct idea of what I mean by unworldliness, than by relating an anecdote of a boy
of rare genius, inheriting genius from both
parents, who, when he began the study of
mathematics, was impressed with so strange
and solemn a sense of awe, that never before,
he said, had he been able to comprehend the
existence of the Eternal.   It is not difficult to
understand what the boy meant.   Mathematics
contain truths entirely independent of Time
and Space; they tell of relations which have
no connection, necessarily, with weight or
quality; they deal with the eternal principles
and laws of the mind; and it is certain, that
these laws are more real and eternal than anything which can be seen or felt.   This is what
I mean by unworldliness: I am not speaking
of it as a theologian, or as a religionist, but I
am speaking of unworldliness in that sense, of
which it is true of all science and high art, as
well as of Nature.   For all high art is essentially unworldliness, and the highest artists
have been unworldly in aim, and unworldly in
life.

Let us compare the life of Benvenuto Cellini. I name him, because there has been given recently to the public a life of him in a popular form. Let us compare his life with the life of Raphael, or Michael Angelo, or Beethoven, or Canova. You will be struck with this difference, that in Benvenuto Cellini there was an entire absence of anything like aspiration beyond the Visible and the Seen ; but in the life of the others there was the strong and perpetual conviction that the things seen were the things unreal, and that the things unseen were the things real ; there was the perpetual desire to realise in a visible form, that beauty which the eye had not seen nor the ear heard, nor which it had ever entered into the heart of man to conceive. I will here quote one single passage in illustration of this ; it is a translation by Wordsworth him-self, from one of the sonnets of Michael Angelo : it is simply an illustration of what I have said :—

" Heaven-born, the soul a heaven-ward course must
    hold ;
   Beyond the visible world she soars to seek
   (For what delights the sense is false and weak)
 Ideal form, the universal mould.
 The wise man, I affirm, can find no rest
   In that which perishes ; nor will he lend
   His heart to aught which doth on time depend."

This is a view of high art : and in this respect

poetry, like high art, and like religion, introduces its votaries into a world of which the
senses take no cognizance; therefore I now
maintain that until a man's eyes have been
clarified by that power which enables him to
look beyond the visible; until—

> " He from thick films shall purge the visual ray,
>   And on the sightless eyeball pour the day."

poetry—high poetry, like Wordsworth's—is
simply and merely unintelligible.

I will give two or three illustrations of the
way in which Wordsworth himself looked on
this subject. The first is in reference to the
power which there is in splendour and in
riches to unfit the mind for the contemplation of invisible and spiritual truths. The
sonnet I am about to read was written in
September, 1802, the period during which the
chief part of the poems I shall read this
evening were written. I believe it was written
to Coleridge.

> " Oh ! friend, I know not which way I must look
>   For comfort, being, as I am, opprest
>   To think that now our life is only drest
> For show ; mean handy-work of craftsman, cook,
> Or groom !—We must run glittering like a brook
>   In the open sunshine, or we are unblest :
> The wealthiest man among us is the best :
>   No grandeur now in nature or in book
>   Delights us."

The connection of these two things is what I wish to fasten your attention upon—

> "The wealthiest man among us is the best,"

that being the spirit of society, then—

> "No grandeur now in nature or in book
> Delights us."

The second illustration is in reference to what is called scandal or gossip. According to Wordsworth, this is the highest manifestation of a worldly spirit. What is it but conversations respecting passing events or passing acquaintances, unappreciated and unelevated by high principle ? Wordsworth has written four sonnets,* worthy of deep study, on this subject. After stating the matter in the first of these, in the second he supposes a possible defence against this habit of general conversation respecting others, derisively.

> " ' Yet life,' you say, 'is life ; we have seen and see
> And with a living pleasure we describe ;
> And fits of sprightly malice do but bribe
> The languid mind into activity.
> Sound sense, and love itself, and mirth and glee,
> Are fostered by the comment and the gibe.' "

Then comes Wordsworth's comment :—

> "Even be it so ; yet still among your tribe,
> Our daily world's true worldlings, rank not me !
> Children are blest and powerful ; their world lies
> More justly balanced ; partly at their feet
> And part far from them : sweetest melodies

---

* *Personal Talk.*

> Are those that are by distance made more sweet.
> Whose mind is but the mind of his own eyes,
> He is a slave ; the meanest we can meet ! "

To understand this, you must carry in your recollection what Wordsworth's views of childhood and infancy are, as given in the sublime "Ode to Immortality." A child, according to Wordsworth, is a being haunted for ever by eternal mind. He tells us that "Heaven lies about us in our infancy"—that the child moves perpetually in two worlds : the world that is seen right before him, and that terminated in another world—a world invisible, the glory of which is as from a palace—"That imperial palace whence he came;" and that high philosophy and poetry are nothing but this coming back to the simple state of childhood, in which we see not merely the thing before us, but the thing before us transfigured and irradiated by the perception of that higher life :—

> "Children are blest and powerful ; their world lies
> More justly balanced ; partly at their feet,
> And part far from them."

Then Wordsworth goes on to show how poetry supplies the place which scandal and gossip had occupied.

> "Dreams, books, are each a world : and books, we know,
> Are a substantial world, both pure and good :
>   Round these, with tendrils strong as flesh and blood,
> Our pastime and our happiness will grow.

> There find I personal themes, a plenteous store,
> Matter wherein right voluble I am,
>> To which I listen with a ready ear ;
>> Two shall be named pre-eminently dear,—
>> The gentle lady married to the Moor ;
> And heavenly Una with her milk-white lamb."

In other words, scandal is nothing more than inverted love of humanity. An absolute necessity, Wordsworth tells us, exists within us for personal themes of conversation that have reference to human beings, and not to abstract principles ; but when that necessity is gratified upon the concerns and occupations of those immediately around us, which necessarily become mixed with envy and evil feelings, then that necessity is inverted and perverted. So the place of detraction or scandal is by the poet occupied by personal themes ; as, for example, when a man has made the object of his household thoughts such characters as Desdemona and Spenser's Una, then he has something which may carry his mind to high and true principles, beyond the present. Then Wordsworth goes on to say,—

> " Nor can I not believe but that hereby
>> Great gains are mine ; for thus I live remote
>> From evil speaking ; rancour, never sought,
> Comes to me not, malignant truth, nor lie.
>> Hence have I genial seasons, hence have I
>>> Smooth passions, smooth discourse, and joyous thought :
>> And thus, from day to day my little boat

Rocks in its harbour, lodging peaceably.
Blessings be with them—and eternal praise,
  Who gave us nobler loves and nobler cares—
  The Poets, who on earth have made us heirs
Of truth and pure delight by heavenly lays."

I shall now read you a passage from a letter written by Wordsworth to Lady Beaumont, in which he answers the objection that his poems were not popular, and explains the reason why in one sense his poetry never could be popular with the world of fashion.

" It is impossible that any expectations can be lower than mine concerning the immediate effect of this little work upon what is called the public. I do not here take into consideration the envy and malevolence, and all the bad passions, which always stand in the way of a work of any merit from a living poet ; but merely think of the pure, absolute, honest, ignorance in which all worldlings of every rank and situation must be enveloped, with respect to the thoughts, feelings, and images, on which the life of my poems depends. The things which I have taken, whether from within or without—what have they to do with routs, dinners, morning calls, hurry from door to door, from street to street, on foot or in carriage ; with Mr Pitt or Mr Fox, Mr Paul or Sir Francis Burdett, the Westminster election or the borough of Honiton ?   In a word—for I cannot

stop to make my way through the hurry of
images that present themselves to me—what
have they to do with endless talking about
things nobody cares anything for, except as far
as their own vanity is concerned, and this with
persons they care nothing for, but as their
vanity or *selfishness* is concerned ?   What have
they to do (to say all at once) with a life
without love ?   In such a life there can be no
thought ;   for we have no thoughts (save
thoughts of pain), but as far as we have love
and admiration.

" It is an awful truth that there neither is, nor
can be, any genuine enjoyment of poetry among
nineteen out of twenty of those persons who
live, or wish to live, in the broad light of the
world—among those who either are, or are
striving to make themselves, people of *consideration* in society.   This is a truth, and an
awful one ;   because to be incapable of a feeling
of poetry, in my sense of the word, is to be
without love of human nature and reverence for
God.

"Upon this I shall insist elsewhere; at present,
let me confine myself to my object, which is to
make you, my dear friend, as easy-hearted as
myself with respect to these poems.   Trouble not
yourself upon their present reception : of what
moment is that, compared with what I trust is
their destiny ?—to console the afflicted ; to add

sunshine to daylight, by making the happy happier; to teach the young and the gracious of every age to see, to think, and feel, and therefore to become more actively and securely virtuous—this is their office, which I trust they will faithfully perform, long after we (that is, all that is mortal of us) are mouldered in our graves."

And then, after some striking criticisms and analyses of his own poetry, he continues :—

"Be assured that the decision of these persons has nothing to do with the question; they are altogether incompetent judges. These people, in the senseless hurry of their idle lives, do not *read* books; they merely snatch a glance at them that they may talk about them. And even if this were not so, never forget what, I believe, was observed to you by Coleridge— that every great and original writer, in proportion as he is great or original, must himself create the taste by which he is to be relished; he must teach the art by which he is to be seen; this, in a certain degree, even to all persons, however wise and pure may be their lives, and however unvitiated their taste. But for those who dip into books in order to give an opinion of them, or talk about them to take up an opinion—for this multitude of unhappy, and misguided, and misguiding beings, an entire regeneration must be produced; and if this be possible, it must be a work *of time.* To conclude, my ears are stone-dead to this idle buzz, and my flesh as insensible as iron to these petty stings; and, after what I have said, I am sure yours will be the same. I doubt not that you will share with me an invincible confidence that my writings (and among them these little poems) will co-operate with the benign tendencies in human nature and society, wherever found; and that they will, in their degree, be efficacious in making men wiser, better, and happier."

In a subsequent letter to Sir George Beaumont, he says, " Let the poet first consult his own heart, as I have done, and leave the rest to posterity—to, I hope, an improving posterity. . . . I have not written down to the level of superficial observers, and unthinking minds. Every great poet is a teacher : I wish either to be considered as a teacher, or nothing."

So far have I tried to prove my point. If my allegations are true, then it follows that a man whose life is choked up by splendour and by riches—a man whose sympathies are perverted by detraction and by gossip—a man whose object is in life to have for himself merely a position in what is called fashionable life—such a man is simply *incapable* of understanding the highest poetry.

The second qualification I shall name for the

appreciation of poetry is, feelings trained and disciplined by the truth of Nature. Let us understand this matter. Poetry represents things, not as they are, but as they seem ; and herein it coincides with all high art, for the difference between science and poetry is this— that science and philosophy endeavour to give to us things as they are, art and poetry represent to us things as they seem. Let us take a simple illustration. The painter represents his distant mountains blue, he gives us the distant circle in the oval of perspective, not because they are so, but because they seem so.

Now, in the same way, just as there are perverted senses to which all things seem unreal, and diseased or morbid senses to which, for example, there is no difference between green and scarlet, and as a man who has represented the glaring and glittering as beautiful, would yet find many who admired him, so, in the same way, in a matter of taste or poetry, there will be found minds perverted by convention, or injured by mere position, to whom Humanity and the Universe will not appear in their true colours, but rather falsely. Mere poets of fashion will have their admirers, just so far as there are those who are found like them, and just so far as their powers are great. For it must be remembered that if a thing seems such to a man, and he has the art of represent-

ing it as it seems, he is a great poet in the first
instance, and if a man has that power to an
eminent degree, he is a greater poet; but the
question whether he is a true poet or not
depends not upon *how* what he represented
appeared to him, but upon the question whether
it *ought* so to have appeared to him, or whether
it does so appear to human nature in its most
unsophisticated and purest mood.   Then comes
the difficulty : what shall be the test ? If things
seem to one man thus, and if they seem to
another man thus, who shall tell us which is
true and which is false poetry, and bring us
back to a standard by which we may determine
what is the judgment of human nature in its
most unsophisticated mood ?   The tests are
two.   The first is feelings disciplined by Nature,
the second is feelings disciplined through the
minds of the acknowledged great masters and
poets.   The first test I have named is feelings
disciplined by Nature ; for as in matters of art,
there are a variety of tastes ; it does not
necessarily follow that there is no real test or
standard of taste.

And just as the real standard is not the
standard of the mass—is not judged by the
majority of votes, but is decided by the few—
so, in matters of poetry, it is not by the mass
or by the majority of votes that these things can
be tested ; but they are to be tested by the

pure, and simple, and true in heart—by those who, all their life long, have been occupied in the discipline of feeling : for in early life poetry is a love, a passion ; we care not for quality, we care only for quantity ; the majesty and pomp of diction delight us ; we love the mere mellifluous flow of the rhyme : and this any one will understand who has heard the boy in the playground spouting, in school-boy phraseology, his sonorous verses.   And so, as life goes on, this passion passes ; the love for poetry wanes, the mystic joy dies with our childhood, and other and more real objects in life and business occupy our attention.   After twenty a man no longer loves poetry passionately, and at fifty or sixty, if you apply to a man for his judgment, you will find it to be that which was his when a boy.   The thirty years that have intervened have been spent in undisciplined feeling, and the taste of the boy is still that of the man— imperfect and undisciplined.

The other test to which I will refer is the judgment of the mind that has been formed on the highest models.   The first test I have spoken of is, of course, Nature seen and felt at first hand ; the second test is Nature seen through the eyes of those who by universal consent are reckoned to have seen Nature best ; and without these it is utterly impossible that a man can judge well.

" These two things, contradictory as they seem, must go together—manly dependence and manly independence, manly reliance and manly self-reliance. Nor can there be given to a thinking man any higher or wiser rule than this—to trust to the judgment of those who from all ages have been reckoned great ; and if he finds that any disparity or difference exists between his judgment and theirs, let him, in all modesty, take it for granted that the fault lies in him and not in them ; for, as a great poet interprets himself to us, he is himself necessary to himself, and we must love him ere to us he will seem worthy of our love." These lines are Wordsworth's, and of no man are they more true than of himself. If you come to Wordsworth in order to find fault, and criticise, and discover passages that can be turned into ridicule or parodied, you will find abundant materials for your mood ; but if, on the other hand, in reliance on the judgment of some of the best and wisest of this age, you will take it for granted that there is something there to learn, and that he can and will teach you how to think and how to feel, I answer for it you will not go away disappointed.

And here lies the great difficulty, the peculiar difficulty of our age ; that it is an age of cant without love, of criticism without reverence. You read the magazines, and the quarterlies, and the daily newspapers, you see some slashing article, and after you have perused that article, in which the claims of some great writer have been discussed cursorily and superficially, you take it for granted that you understand, and can form a judgment upon the matter ; and yet, all the while, very likely that article has been written by some clever, flippant young man, to whom, for his own misfortune and for the misfortune of the public, the literary department has been committed.   What we want is the old spirit of our forefathers ; the firm conviction that not by criticism, but by sympathy, we must understand : what we want is more reverence, more love, more humanity, more depth.

The third qualification I shall name for an appreciation of poetry is, a certain delicacy and depth of feeling.   I do not say that this is necessary for all poets,—nay, even for some of the highest it is not necessary ; for the epic poet appeals to all minds, he describes things which are applicable to all ; the dramatic poet appeals to all, because, although unquestionably some of his characters move in an atmosphere that is unintelligible to the mass, yet in the multi-plicity of characters he produces there must be a majority that are intelligible to all ; the poet of passion appeals to all, because passions are common to us all.   It does not require, for example, much delicacy or profoundness to understand and feel the writings of Anacreon Moore ; but there are poets who give us truths which none can appreciate but those who have been engaged in watching faithfully the order in which feelings succeed each other, the successions of our inner life, the way in which things appear in this world when presented to our mind in our highest state. No man needs this discipline and preparation more than the student of Wordsworth, for he gives to us the subtle and pure and delicate and refined succession of human feelings, of which the mind is scarcely conscious, except at the moment when the figure is before us, and we are listening with stilled breath to the mysterious march of our inner life.

I will now proceed to give you a few examples of this ; but you will observe that I labour under peculiar disadvantages in doing so ; for just in proportion as thoughts are delicate, and refined, and subtle, exactly in the same proportion are they unfit for public exposition : they may be fitted for the closet, the study, and for private reading, but they are not fitted for a public room ; therefore, the most exquisite productions of Wordsworth I shall not bring before you now ; all I shall read to you will be some that will give you a conception of what I have stated. For example, I quote one passage in which the

poet describes the consecrating effects of early
dawn :—

> " What soul was his when from the naked top
>   Of some bold headland he beheld the sun
>   Rise up and bathe the world in light ! He look'd—
>   Ocean and earth, the solid frame of earth
>   And ocean's liquid mass, beneath him lay
>   In gladness and deep joy. The clouds were touch'd,
>   And in their silent faces did he read
>   Unutterable love. Sound needed none,
>   Nor any voice of joy ; his spirit drank
>   The spectacle ; sensation, soul, and form
>   All melted into him ; They swallowed up
>   His animal being ; In them did he live,
>   And by them did he live ; They were his life.
>   In such access of mind, in such high hour
>   Of visitation from the Living God.
>   Thought was not ; in enjoyment it expired :
>   No thanks he breathed, he proffered no request :
>   Rapt into still communion that transcends
>   The imperfect offices of prayer and praise,
>   His mind was a thanksgiving to the Power
>   That made him ; it was blessedness and love ! "

There is nothing in these lines except we
have the heart to feel them. No man can
understand or feel those lines who has led a
slothful life, or who has not at one time or
other loved to rise early,—no man who, in his
early walks, has not mingled with a love of
poetry a deep religious sense, who has not felt
the consecrating effects of early dawn, or who has
not at one time or another, in his early days, in a
moment of deep enthusiasm, knelt down amidst

the glories of Nature, as the ancient patriarch
knelt, canopied only by the sky above him, and
feeling that none were awake but the Creator
and himself,—bowed down to consecrate and
offer up the whole of his life, experiencing also
a strange, and awful, and mysterious feeling,
as if a Hand invisible was laid upon his brow,
accepting the consecration and the sacrifice.

In order to understand the next passage I
shall quote, I must remind you of the way in
which the ancient Pagans represented the same
feeling.   Most persons here, either through the
originals, if they are acquainted with them, or
through the translations, which in these times
have multiplied, will remember how the ancient
Pagan poets loved to represent some anecdote
of a huntsman or shepherd, who, in passing
through a wood and plucking some herb or
cutting down some branch, has started to see
drops of human blood issue from it, or at
hearing a human voice proclaiming that he had
done injury to some imprisoned human life in
that tree.   It was so that the ancients expressed their feelings of the deep sacredness of
that life that there is in Nature.   Now, let us
see how Wordsworth expresses this.   As usual,
and as we might have expected, he brings it
before us by a simple anecdote of his childhood,
when he went out nutting.   He tells us how,
in early boyhood, he went out to seek for nuts,

and came to a hazel-tree set far in the thicket
of a wood, which never had been entered by the
profane steps of boyhood before—as he expresses it, "A virgin scene." He describes how
he eyed with delight the clusters of white nuts
hanging from the branches, and with exquisite
fidelity to nature,—he tells us how he sat upon
a bank and dallied with the promised feast, as
we sometimes dally with a letter we have long
expected, and which we know is now our own.
At last the boy rose, tore down the boughs, and
on seeing all the ravage and desolation he had
caused by his intrusion, there came over him
a feeling of deep remorse.

> "And unless I now
> Confound my present feelings with the past ;
> Ere from the mutilated bower I turned
> Exulting, rich beyond the wealth of kings,
> I felt a sense of pain when I beheld
> The silent trees, and saw the intruding sky.—
> Then, dearest maiden, move along these shades
> In gentleness of heart ; with gentle hand
> Touch—for there is a spirit in the wood."

I preface the third illustration that I shall
offer, by a remark reminding you that these
scenes of Nature become, as it were, a possession
of the memory. The value of having felt
Nature in her loveliness or in her grandeur is
not in the pleasure and intense enjoyment that
was then and there experienced, but in this
fact, that we have thenceforward gained some-

thing that will not be put aside ; a remembrance that will form a great part of our future life. Now, all of us,—any man who has seen the Alps, or who has seen an American hurricane, can understand this so far as Nature's grandeur is concerned ; but Wordsworth, as usual, shows us how our daily life and most ordinary being is made up of such recollections ; and, as usual, he selects a very simple anecdote to illustrate this : it is taken from a circumstance that occurred to him when on a journey with his sister on the lake of Ullswater ; they came upon a scene which, perhaps, few but himself would have observed.   The margin of the lake was fringed for a long distance with golden daffodils,

> " Fluttering and dancing in the breeze."

And then, after describing this in very simple language, these lines occur :—

> " The waves beside them danced ; but they
> Out-did the sparkling waves in glee :
> A poet could not but be gay,
> In such a jocund company :
> I gazed—and gazed—but little thought
> What wealth the show to me had brought :

> " For oft, when on my couch I lie.
> In vacant or in pensive mood,
> They flash upon that inward eye,
> Which is the bliss of solitude ;
> And then my heart with pleasure fills,
> And dances with the daffodils."

Now, I will give you a specimen of shallow criticism. In a well-known *Review* for the current quarter there is a review of Wordsworth; and among other passages there is one in which the reviewer, with a flippancy which characterizes the whole of the article, remarks that the passage which has just been read is nothing more than a versified version of a certain entry in Miss Wordsworth's journal. How stands the fact? It is unquestionably true that there was an entry in Miss Wordsworth's journal, written in very striking prose, of the same sight which her brother and herself had seen; it is quite true that the first two stanzas and the greater part of the third were nothing more than Miss Wordsworth's very beautiful prose put into very beautiful verse. So far then, if you strike off the last stanza and the two lines of the stanza preceding it, you have nothing more than a versified version of the entry in Miss Wordsworth's journal; but then, the last stanza contains the very idea of all, towards which all tended, and without which the piece would not have been poetry at all. What would you think of a man who denied to Shakspere the praise of originality, on the ground that his plays were chiefly constructed from some ancient chronicler, Holingshed, for example, or taken from the plot of some old play, and that in every play he had incorporated some hundred lines of the old play? What has Shakspere added? Only the *genius :* he has only added the breath and life which made the dry bones of the skeleton live. What has Wordsworth added? He has added nothing except the *poetry :* nothing but the thought, the one lovely thought, which redeems the whole.

Now, I have quoted the passages you have heard, in order to call your attention to the subtle perception and the exquisite delicacy which is in them. I have reminded you of the difficulty I encounter in bringing them before a public audience. In reading Wordsworth the sensation is as the sensation of the pure water drinker, whose palate is so refined that he can distinguish between rill and rill, river and river, fountain and fountain, as compared with the obtuser sensation of him who has destroyed the delicacy of his palate by grosser libations, and who can distinguish no difference between water and water, because to him all pure things are equally insipid. It is like listening to the mysterious music in the conch sea shell, which is so delicate and refined that we are uncertain whether it is the music and sound of the shell, or merely the pulses throbbing in our own ear ; it is like watching the quivering rays of fleeting light that shoot up to heaven as we are looking at the sunset ; so fine, so exquisitely touching is the sense of feeling, that we doubt whether it is reality we are gazing upon at all, or whether it is not merely an image created by the power and the trembling of our own inner imagination.

I will pass on, now, in the second place, to consider the life of Wordsworth, so far as it may be considered to have affected his poetry. We all know that Wordsworth was remarkable for certain theories of poetry, which, in his time, when they first appeared, were considered new, heterodox, heretical. On a future occasion I hope to examine these; at present, I am bound to endeavour to investigate the question, how far Wordsworth's life and Wordsworth's character may be supposed to have formed, or, at all events, modified, these conclusions.

Now, first of all, I will remark that Wordsworth's was a life of contemplation, not of action, and therein differed from Arnold's of Rugby. Arnold of Rugby is the type of English action; Wordsworth is the type of English thought. If you look at the portraits of the two men, you will distinguish this difference. In one there is concentrativeness, energy, proclaimed; in the eye of the other there is vacancy, dreaminess. The life of Wordsworth was the life of a recluse. In these days it is the fashion to talk of the dignity of work as the one sole aim and end of human life, and foremost in proclaiming this as a great truth we find Thomas Carlyle. Every

man who pretends in any degree to have
studied the manifold tendencies of this age will
be familiar with the writings of Carlyle, and
there can be no man who has studied them who
does not recollect the vivid and eloquent passage
in which Carlyle speaks of the sacredness of
work. Now, it appears to me, that this word is
passing almost into cant among the disciples of
Carlyle ; and even with Carlyle himself in
these Latter-day pamphlets, in which he speaks
of everything and every one not engaged in
present work, as if the sooner they were out of
this work-a-day world the better. In opposition to this, I believe that as the vocation of
some is naturally work, so the vocation, the
heaven-born vocation of others, is naturally
contemplation.

In very early times human life was divided
into seven parts, whereof six were given to
work and one to rest, and both of these were
maintained equally sacred—sacred work and
sacred rest ; and it is not uprooting that great
principle, but carrying it out in its spirit, to say
—that as of the seven parts of human life the
majority belonged to work, so should a fraction
be dedicated to rest ; that though it is true of
the majority that the life-law is work, yet it is
also true that there is a fraction to whom by
nature the life-law is the law of contemplation.
But let no one suppose that contemplation, in the

Wordsworthian sense of the word, is listlessness
or inaction.　There is a sweat of the brain,
and a sweat of the heart, be well assured—
working-men especially—as much as there is
a sweat of the brow ; and contemplation, in
Wordsworth's sense of the word, is the dedicat-
ing a life to the hard and severe inner work of
brain : it is the retiring from the world, in order
to fit the spirit to do its work.

Let us understand what this work was which
Wordsworth proposed to himself.　At the
period when Wordsworth came upon the stage,
there were two great tendencies—and, in some
respects, evil tendencies—which civilisation and
modern society were beginning to develop.
The first of these was the accumulation of
wealth ; the second was the division of labour.

I am not going to speak of the accumulation
of wealth as a fanatic.　I know some who say
with reference to wealth and capital, that
wealth is a necessary ingredient in the produc-
tion of things, of which labour is the other
ingredient, and without which labour will be
altogether useless.　I know that no nation has
ever risen to greatness without accumulated
capital ; and yet, notwithstanding this, there
is a crisis in the history of nations—and a
dangerous crisis it is—when the aristocracy of
birth has been succeeded by the aristocracy of
wealth : and a great historian tells us, that no

nation has ever yet reached that crisis, without having *already* begun its downward progress towards deterioration.

There are chiefly, I believe, three influences counter-active of that great danger, accumulated wealth. The first is religion, the second is hereditary rank, and the third is the influence of men of contemplative lives. The first is religion, of which, as belonging to another place, for the sake of reverence, I will not speak here. The second counteracting influence to accumulated wealth is hereditary rank. It is not generally the fashion in the present day to speak highly of rank, much less before the members of an Athenæum or of a Working Man's Institute; it is the fashion, rather, to speak of our common Humanity, and to deprecate Rank; and good and right it is that common Humanity should be dignified, and elevated far above the distinction of convention and all the arbitrary and artificial differences of class; and yet, after all this, in an age when it certainly is not the fashion to speak well of hereditary rank, it is well for us all to remember the advantages that have accrued to us in the past, from that hereditary rank. I will say that Rank is a power in itself more spiritual, because less tangible, than the power of wealth. The man who commands others by the extent of his broad acres, or by the number of his bales of cotton, rules them by a power more degrading and more earthly than he who rules them simply by the *prestige* of long hereditary claims.

You all remember how well Sir Walter Scott has described this power as existing more strongly among the Highlanders of Scotland than in any other nation. In the " Fair Maid of Perth," for example, in the contest between the clans, you will remember how every clansman dedicated himself to certain death for the sake of his chieftain, and how a young man, with no wealth, unknown before, nay, having in himself no intrinsic worth or goodness, obtained a loyalty and devotion that royalty itself could scarcely win ; a devotion and love that all the wealth of the burghers of Perth never could have purchased : and you feel that so long as there was such a power in Scotland it was impossible that the burghers of Perth, with all their wealth, could obtain undisputed predominancy. So long as this power exists, the power of wealth has something to be thrown in the scale against it ; and therefore it is that, with feelings strong on the side of human progress, and with but little reverence for mushroom rank, I am yet free to acknowledge that I feel sometimes a pang, when I hear or read of the extinction of great names, grey with the hoar of innumerable ages—sorrow, when I read in paper after paper of the passing of

great ancestral estates under the hammer of
the auctioneer ; and for this reason, that in
every such case I feel that there is one more
sword gone that would have helped us in the
battle which we must all fight against the
superstitious idolatry of Wealth.

The third counteracting influence is the
existence of men of contemplative minds—
men of science and philosophy. You may call
them useless ; but they are men whose vocation
elevates them above the existing world, and
makes them indifferent to show and splendour,
and therefore they can throw their influence
and weight in the scale against the aristocracy
of wealth. The other evil I have spoken of, I
called the division of labour : and here, again,
I speak not as a fanatic. Political economists,
Adam Smith, for example, tell us that in the
fabrication of a pin, from ten to eighteen men
are required. One cuts the wire, another draws
it, a third points it, three are required to make
the head, another to polish it, and it is a
separate work even to put the pin into the
paper. And now, we know the advantage of
all this.

The political economist tells us, that ten
such men working together can make in a
single day forty or fifty thousand pins, whereas,
had they worked separately, they could scarcely
have made ten. We all know the advantage

of this; we know that a man becomes more expert by directing his whole attention to one particular branch of a trade than by wasting it on many; we know that time is thus saved, which would otherwise be spent in going from one work to another; we know that the inventive faculty is consequently quickened, because a man who is for ever considering one subject only, is also enabled to occupy his attention with the thought as to how the operation can be most simplified. These are great advantages; yet no man can persuade me that with these advantages there are not also great disadvantages to the *inner life* of the man so engaged. We get a perfect pin, but we get most imperfect *men*, for while one man is engaged in polishing the pin, and another is engaged in sharpening it, what have we? We have nothing more in the man than a pin-polisher; we have sacrificed the man to the pin.

In some of the States of Western America, we are told of men who, by the very facts of their position, are compelled to clear their own ground, to sow and reap it with their own hands, to thatch and build their own cottages, and to break and shoe their own horses, and who give a great deal of attention, notwithstanding, to the consideration of great questions, commercial and political. This is, no doubt, an imperfect society, for everything is

incomplete; and yet travellers tell us that
there are nowhere such specimens of Humanity;
that the men have not only large brains and
large muscles, but both these joined together.
On the one hand, then, we have a more complete society and a less complete individual;
on the other hand, we have a more complete
individual and a less complete society. This is
the disadvantage, this is the high price we must
pay for all civilisation and progress; in the
words of Tennyson, "The individual withers
and the world is more and more." And, then,
life is so divided; we have the dentist and the
oculist, but they are only the dentist and the
oculist; we have the clergyman and the
farmer, but the farmer knows nothing of the
clergyman; and is it not a charge brought
against the clergy at this very moment, that
they are clergymen and nothing more?

No man felt these two dangers more than
Wordsworth felt them; he felt himself called
upon to do battle against the evils of his age;
he acknowledged that he had received a commission and consecration; he was, as we have
already heard, "a consecrated spirit:" and yet
he took a fair and just measure of his own
powers; he knew well that his work was not to
be done on the platform, in the pulpit, or in the
senate. He retired to his own mountains, and
there, amidst the regenerating influences of

nature, where all was real, he tried to discipline his own heart in order that he might be enabled to look calmly and truly on the manifold aspects of human life. And from that solitude there came from time to time a calm clear voice, calling his countrymen back to simplicity and truth, proclaiming the dignity and the simplicity in feeling of our primitive nature : in opposition to the superstitious idolatry of wealth, proclaiming from time to time that a man's life consists not in the abundance of the things he possesses : in opposition to the danger arising from divided employment and occupations, proclaiming the sanctity of each separate human soul, and asserting, in defiance of the manufacturer, who called men "hands," that every man was not a "hand," but a living soul.

It was in this way that Wordsworth advocated the truth of poetry. He did a great, and high, and holy work, the value of which must not be calculated nor measured by his success, but by its truth. The work Wordsworth did, and I say it in all reverence, was the work which the Baptist did when he came to the pleasure-laden citizens of Jerusalem to work a reformation ; it was the work which Milton tried to do, when he raised that clear, calm voice of his to call back his countrymen to simpler manners and to simpler laws. That was what Wordsworth did, or tried to do ; and the language in which

he has described Milton might with great truth
be applied to Wordsworth himself :—

> " Milton ! thou should'st be living at this hour :
> England hath need of thee : she is a fen
> Of stagnant waters : altar, sword, and pen,
> Fireside, the heroic wealth of hall and bower,
> Have forfeited their ancient English dower
> Of inward happiness.   We are selfish men ;
> Oh ! raise us up, return to us again ;
> And give us manners, virtue, freedom, power,
> Thy soul was like a star, and dwelt apart :
> Thou hadst a voice whose sound was like the sea :
> Pure as the naked heavens, majestic, free.
> So didst thou travel on life's common way,
> In cheerful godliness ; and yet thy heart
> The lowliest duties on herself did lay."

I will now read to you one or two passages in
which Wordsworth shows the power of this life
of contemplation.   The first I shall read is one
written by Wordsworth soon after the Convention of Cintra.   According to Wordsworth's
view, England had been guilty in that Convention of great selfishness.   It appeared to
Wordsworth that, instead of using the opportunity given her to ransom Portugal and Spain,
she had consulted her own selfishness, and
allowed her enemy, the French, to escape with
a retreat almost equal to victory.   In consequence of this, Wordsworth wrote a tract, in
one passage of which he defended himself
for pretending to judge of such matters :—
He says, " The evidence to which I have made

appeal, in order to establish the truth, is not locked up in cabinets, but is accessible to all ; as it exists in the bosoms of men—in the appearances and intercourse of daily life—in the details of passing events—and in general history. And more especially in its right import within the reach of him who, taking no part in public measures, and having no concern in the changes of things but as they affect what is most precious in his country and humanity, will doubtless be more alive to those genuine sensations which are the materials of sound judgment. Nor is it to be overlooked, that such a man may have more leisure (and probably will have a stronger inclination) to communicate with the records of past ages."

I will take one other passage, in which, judging of the affairs of Spain with almost perfect nicety, Wordsworth again appealed to the power and right given to him, by contemplation, to judge of such a subject :—

> " Not mid the world's vain objects, that enslave
>   The free-born soul—that world whose vaunted skill
>   In selfish interest perverts the will,
>   Whose factions lead astray the wise and brave—
>   Not there ; but in dark wood, and rocky cave,
>   And hollow vale, which foaming torrents fill
>   With omnipresent murmur as they rave
>   Down their steep beds, that never shall be still :
>   Here, mighty nature ! in this school sublime,
>   I weigh the hopes and fears of suffering Spain,

For her consult the auguries of time ;
And through the human heart explore my way,
And look and listen—gathering, whence I may,
Triumph and thoughts no bondage can restrain."

The second great feature in Wordsworth's
life and history was his fidelity to himself.
Early in life he felt himself a consecrated spirit,
bound to be such, else sinning greatly. He
said that he made no vows, but that, unknown
to him, vows were made for him. Wordsworth
felt that he had what we call in modern times a
vocation or a mission, and no man was ever
more true to his vocation than Wordsworth : he
was not disobedient to the heavenly vision ; he
recognised the voice within him and obeyed it ;
and no wish for popularity, no dazzling invita-
tions to a brighter life, could ever make him
break his vows or leave his solitude. The
generosity of a few private friends,—Calvert,
Beaumont, Lord Lonsdale,—enabled him to
live in retirement ; but when he was afterwards
invited to leave his seclusion for a town life he
refused, because he felt that that would destroy
the simplicity he was cultivating.

Wordsworth was no copyist ; upon himself
he formed himself. He took no model ; he
took the powers and light which were in him,
and worked them out. This will account for
what some writers called the fanatical egotism
of the Lake writers. Egotism, if you will ; but

there is many a man who is wasting his energies who has, nevertheless, the power within him to be something, if he will only not try to be something which he cannot be—if he will only be content to be what he is within himself, instead of aiming at some model it is impossible for him ever to realise.   Abstractedly, no doubt, the armour of the warrior was better than the sling of the shepherd ; but for the shepherd the shepherd's sling was best.   And so Wordsworth worked out his history, destiny, and life ; and, after all, when you look at it, in his case, it was not egotism.   Wordsworth said that he made no vows ; vows were made for him.   And here is the difference between the egotist and the humility of the great man : the egotist is ever speaking and thinking of that which belongs to himself alone and comes from himself ; but the great man, when speaking of himself, or thinking of himself, is convinced that which is in him is not his own, but a Voice to which he must listen, and to which, at his peril, he must yield obedience.   There has ever been to me something exceedingly sublime in the spectacle of Wordsworth, through obloquy, through long years, through contempt, still persevering in his calm, consistent course—something sublime in those expressions which afterwards turned out to be a prophecy, in which, indifferent to present popularity, he looked towards the future.   His friends, who loved him, his brothers, who adored him, were unsatisfied with the public opinion. " Make yourselves at rest respecting me," said Wordsworth ; " I speak the truths the world must feel at last."   There are not many passages in Wordsworth's Works that bear upon his feelings during this time, and there is only one passage I will read to you now.   It is that ode he wrote to Haydon :—

> " High is our calling, friend !—Creative art
> (Whether the instrument of words she use,
> Or pencil pregnant with ethereal hues,)
> Demands the service of a mind and heart,
> Though sensitive, yet, in their weakest part,
> Heroically fashioned—to infuse
> Faith in the whispers of the lonely muse,
> While the whole world seems adverse to desert.
> And, oh ! when nature sinks, as oft she may,
> Through long-lived pressure of obscure distress,
> Still to be strenuous for a bright reward,
> And in the soul admit of no decay,
> Brook no continuance of weak-mindedness :
> Great is the glory, for the strife is hard !"

This brings me to consider Wordsworth in his success as a poet.   The cause of Wordsworth, which was desperate once, is triumphant now ; and yet it is well to look back to fifty years ago, and to remember how it was with him then. Wordsworth's biographer informs us that between 1807 and 1815 there was not one edition of his works called for.   The different reviews sneered at him, Jeffrey lashed him, Byron tried to annihilate him ; and it was in reference to some such attempt of Byron that Southey said, " He crush the Excursion ! he might as well attempt to crush Mount Skiddaw ! " It was about that time that Fox returned a calm, cold, unsympathising answer to the enclosure of a volume of Wordsworth's poems which Wordsworth had sent ; and then also occurred one circumstance which is full of significance. Cottle, the bookseller, of Bristol, made over his stock and effects to the Messrs Longman, and it was necessary to take an inventory of the stock, and in that inventory was found one volume noted down as worth "*nil.*" That volume contained the lyric poems of Wordsworth ; and it may be well, also, to say that it contained first of all Coleridge's poem of the Ancient Mariner, and afterwards those exquisite lines of Wordsworth on Revisiting Tintern Abbey.

Thirty years after this, the then Prime Minister of England, Sir Robert Peel, in a letter full of dignified, and touching, and graceful feeling, proffered to Wordsworth the Laureateship of England ; acknowledging, in addition, that though he had mentioned the subject not to few, but to many persons, and not to men of small, but to men of great reputation, there was but one unanimous opinion, that the selection was the only one that could be made.

I remember myself one of the most public

exhibitions of this change in public feeling.   It was my lot, during a short university career, to witness a transition and a reaction, or revulsion, of public feeling, with respect to two great men whom I have already mentioned and contrasted. The first of these was one who was every inch a man—Arnold of Rugby.   You will all recollect how in his earlier life Arnold was covered with suspicion and obloquy ; how the wise men of his day charged him with latitudinarianism, and I know not with how many other heresies.   But the public opinion altered, and he came to Oxford and read lectures on Modern History. Such a scene had not been seen in Oxford before.   The lecture-room was too small ; all adjourned to the Oxford theatre ; and all that was most brilliant, all that was most wise and most distinguished, gathered together there. He walked up to the rostrum with a quiet step and manly dignity.   Those who had loved him when all the world despised him, felt that, at last, the hour of their triumph had come.   But there was something deeper than any personal triumph they could enjoy ; and those who saw him then will not soon forget the lesson read to them by his calm, dignified, simple step,—a lesson teaching them the utter worthlessness of unpopularity or of popularity as a test of manhood's worth.

The second occasion was when, in the same

theatre, Wordsworth came forward to receive his honorary degree. Scarcely had his name been pronounced, than from three thousand voices at once, there broke forth a burst of applause, echoed and taken up again and again when it seemed about to die away, and that thrice repeated—a cry in which

"Old England's heart and voice unite,
   Whether she hail the wine cup or the fight,
   Or bid each hand be strong, or bid each heart be light."

There were young eyes there, filled with an emotion of which they had no need to be ashamed; there were hearts beating with the proud feeling of triumph, that, at last, the world had recognised the merit of the man they had loved so long, and acknowledged as their teacher; and yet, when that noise was protracted, there came a reaction in their feelings, and they began to perceive that *that* was not, after all, the true reward and recompense for all that Wordsworth had done for England : it seemed as if all that noise was vulgarizing the poet ; it seemed more natural and desirable, to think of him afar off in his simple dales and mountains, the high priest of Nature, weaving in honoured poverty his songs to liberty and truth, than to see him there clad in a scarlet robe and be-spattered with applause. Two young men went home together, part of the way in silence, and one only gave expression to the feelings of the other when he quoted those well-known, trite, and often-quoted lines,—lines full of deepest truth—

> " The self-approving hour whole worlds outweighs
> Of stupid starers and of loud huzzas :
> And more true joy Marcellus exiled feels
> Than Cæsar with a senate at his heels."

The last thing I shall remark on respecting Wordsworth's life was Wordsworth's consistency.   I shall here quote a passage in which he alludes to the change brought against him of having deserted his former opinions.   " I should think that I had lived to little purpose if my notions on the subject of government had undergone no modification : my youth must, in that case, have been without enthusiasm, and my manhood endued with small capability of profiting by reflection.   If I were addressing those who have dealt so liberally with the words renegade, apostate, etc., I should retort the charge upon them, and say, *you* have been deluded by *places* and *persons*, while I have stuck to *principles*."   It may appear to many persons a desperate thing to defend Wordsworth's consistency in the very teeth of facts ; for it is unquestionable that in his early life Wordsworth was a Republican, and sympathized with the French Revolution, and that in his later life he wrote lines of stern condemnation for its excesses.   It is unquestionable, moreover, that in

early life Wordsworth rebelled against anything
like ecclesiastical discipline ; that he could not
even bear the morning and evening prayers at
chapel, and yet that in later life he wrote a
large number of Ecclesiastical sonnets, of which
I will at present only quote one on Archbishop
Laud—

> "Prejudged by foes determined not to spare
>   An old weak man for vengeance thrown aside,
>   Laud, 'in the painful art of dying' tried,
>   (Like a poor bird entangled in a snare,
>   Whose heart still flutters, though his wings forbear
>   To stir in useless struggle), hath relied
>   On hope that conscious innocence supplied,
>   And in his prison breathes celestial air.
>   Why tarries then thy chariot ? wherefore stay,
>   O Death ! the ensanguined yet triumphant wheels,
>   Which thou preparest, full often to convey
>   (What time a state with maddening faction reels)
>   The saint or patriot to the world that heals
>   All wounds, all perturbations doth allay." *

* Wordsworth appended to this sonnet the following note,
which is given entire to show the strength of his opinion on this
subject :—

"In this age a word cannot be said in praise of Laud, or
even in compassion for his fate, without incurring a charge of
bigotry ; but fearless of such imputation, I concur with Hume,
'that it is sufficient for his vindication to observe that his errors
were the most excusable of all those which prevailed during
that zealous period.' A key to the right understanding of those
parts of his conduct that brought the most odium upon him in
his own time, may be found in the following passage of his
speech before the bar of the House of Peers : 'Ever since I
came in place, I have laboured nothing more than that the external publick worship of God, so much slighted in divers parts

So that Wordsworth began as a Republican and ended as a Tory ; he began in defiance of everything ecclesiastical, and ended as a High Churchman. This change has been viewed by persons of different parties with different sentiments. To some, as to the poet Shelley, it appeared an apostacy from the purity of his earlier principles ; to others, as if the sacredness of his earlier principles had been ripened with the mellowed strength of manly life. Among these last is his biographer, Dr Wordsworth ; and it is curious to see what pains he has taken to point to some passage by which the evil of another might be modified—aiming at one great and chief object, namely, to prove that Wordsworth died a Tory and a High Churchman. Be it so : I am prepared to say that the inner life of Wordsworth was consistent. In order to prove this, let us bear in mind that there are two kinds of truth—the one is the truth of fact, the other is ideal truth : and these are not one, they are often opposite to each other. For example, when the agriculturist sees a small white almond-like thing rising from the ground,

of this kingdom, might be preserved, and that with as much decency and uniformity as might be. For I evidently saw, that the publick neglect of God's service in the outward face of it, and the nasty lying of many places dedicated to that service, *had almost cast a damp upon the true and inward worship of God, which, while we live in the body, needs external helps, and all little enough to keep it in any vigour.*"

he calls that an oak ; but that is not a truth of fact, it is an ideal truth.   The oak is a large tree, with spreading branches, and leaves, and acorns ; but that is only a thing an inch long, and imperceptible in all its development ; yet the agriculturist sees in it the idea of what it shall be, and, if I may borrow a scriptural phrase, he *imputes* to it the majesty, and excellence, and glory, that is to be hereafter.

Let us carry this principle into the change of Wordsworth's principles.   In early life Wordsworth was a democrat : an admirer of the French Revolution : he sympathised deeply, manfully, with the cause of the poor ; he loved them, and desired their elevation.   But he sympathised with them as the stately nobles of nature ; he saw in them, not what they were, but what they might be ; and in all Wordsworth's pedlars, and broom-gatherers, and gipsies, and wanderers, we have not bad men, defiled by crime ; but there is, speaking through them all, the high, pure mind of Wordsworth.   He simply exhibited his own humanity, which he felt and knew to be in them also.   This is an ideal truth and not a truth of fact, and the idea is not what they were, but what they ought to be, and what they yet should be.

Let us, again, on the other hand, come to the question of Wordsworth's change into High Churchism and Toryism.   And first, by the way,

I would remark that there is another side of the truth Wordsworth put forward, which you will find in a poem familiar to most of you, in which Canning has given us the history of the " Needy Knife Grinder." A republican, in all the warmth of republican spirit, with his lips full of liberty, fraternity, and equality, sees approaching, a man in rags—a poor wretched looking being ; and he instantly imagines that here is some victim to the oppression of the Poor Laws, the Game Laws, or of Tithes, or Taxation ; but it turns out, upon inquiry, that he has before him a man of bad life, of indolent and intemperate habits, who, in a fit of intoxication, has got into the wretched state in which he beholds him ; and the indignation and confusion of our good republican are completed when the Needy Knife Grinder entreats that he would give him some small coin, in order that he might become drunk again. This is the other side of truth—the truth of fact—a low, and base, and vulgar truth. And, after all, when we come to examine these, which is the higher truth ?—is it higher to state things as they really are, or to state them as they ought to be ?—to say that the lower classes are degraded, and evil, and base ; or to say that there yet slumbers in them the aristocratic and the godlike, and that *that*, by the grace of God, shall one day be drawn forth ? In early life, then, in all his most democratic feelings, Wordsworth was an aristocrat at heart.

And now we come to the other side of the question. And first, in reference to the term "High Churchism," I do not use it in an offensive sense. If there are any persons here holding High Church views, I implore them to believe that, although I am not a High Churchman myself—far from it—I can yet sympathise with them in all their manliness and high-mindedness; and recognise much in them that is pure and aspiring. If, therefore, I now give my own definition of High Churchism, let them not be offended. There are, then, two things opposite to each other; the one is Pantheism, the other is High Churchism. Pantheism is a tendency to see the god-like everywhere, the personal God nowhere. The other, is the tendency to localize the personal Deity in certain places, certain times, and certain acts; certain places called consecrated churches; certain times called fast-days, and so forth; certain acts, called acts of ecclesiastical life, in certain persons, called consecrated priests. These two things, you will observe, are opposed to each other—diametrically opposed. Now, it is a strange and remarkable fact, that Wordsworth has been charged with both these things; by some he has been charged with Pantheism, and by others with what we call High Churchism.

In reference to Pantheism, in order that those who are not familiar with the word may understand it, I will quote one or two passages from Wordsworth. The first, which occurs in the sonnets, I have read. In that it will be seen that Wordsworth speaks of the force of Nature as if that were the only living Soul of the world. I will take another passage which occurs in the well-known lines on Revisiting Tintern Abbey:—

> "And I have felt
> A presence that disturbs me with the joy
> Of elevated thoughts ; a sense sublime
> Of something far more deeply interfused,
> Whose dwelling is the light of setting suns,
> And the round ocean, and the living air,
> And the blue sky, and in the mind of man:
> A Motion and a Spirit, that impels
> All thinking things, all objects of all thought,
> And rolls through all things."

In these words, grand and magnificent as they are, we have the very germ of Pantheism. But now, in looking at one of these classes of passages, we must ever remember to modify it by the other. When Wordsworth spoke as a High Churchman, we must remember that he was the very same man who spoke of the living Being that created the universe, as " A Motion and a Spirit that impels all thinking things ; " and when, on the other hand, he uses language which seems to pass almost into Pantheism, we must remember that he was the same man who

wrote the Ecclesiastical sonnets, and who spoke
of a personal and localized Deity.

And what if it be true,—and true it is,—that
the earlier part of Wordsworth's life was characterised by the predominancy of one of these
feelings, and the later part by the other—is
there anything there that is unnatural or incon-
sistent? Is it natural if the mind of a man pro-
gresses from the vague transcendental down
towards the personal? Is there anything incon-
sistent in the great truth, that the mind of man,
after having wandered in the outer confines of the
circumference of this universe, should at last
seek its home and find its blessedness in the rest
of a personal centre? Now, with respect to the
other point namely, Wordsworth's Toryism, or
Conservatism—call it what you will : it does not
matter whether I am now addressing Tories or
Radicals; since we are speaking of great principles
we will have done with names. I will read you
a passage in which Wordsworth speaks of
England :—

> " Hail to the crown by freedom shaped—to gird
> An English sovereign's brow ! and to the throne
> Whereon he sits.   Whose deep foundations lie
> In veneration and the people's love ;
> Whose steps are equity, whose seal is law."

Now, the veriest democrat can only object to
this as a matter of fact, and will probably say,
" If this be England I would desire to preserve

her as she is ; but because I do not believe it, I
desire to alter her : in heart and in idea we are
one, the only point on which we differ is the
point of historical fact." I say, therefore, that
in Wordsworth's most democratic days he was
aristocratic in heart ; and in his most aristocratic
days he had all that was most generous, and all
that was most aspiring in the democratic mind.
I now come rapidly towards the conclusion ;
but having said what I have, it is necessary that
I should complete the picture by giving you an
idea of the patriotism in Wordsworth ; that
intense and deep love for England, in which
aristocrat and democrat are blended in the
formation of one high-minded man. I will read
a passage showing Wordsworth's love for his
country :—

> "When I have borne in memory what has tamed
>   Great nations, how ennobling thoughts depart
>   When men change swords for ledgers, and desert
> The student's bower for gold, some fears unnamed
> I had, my country !—am I to be blamed,
>   Now, when I think of thee, and what thou art,
>   Verily in the bottom of my heart,
> Of those unfilial fears I am ashamed.
>   For dearly must we prize thee ; we who find
> In thee a bulwark for the cause of men ;
>   And I by my affection was beguiled :
> What wonder if a poet now and then,
>   Among the many movements of his mind,
> Felt for thee as a lover or a child ?"

I must preface the next sonnet I have to

read, by reminding you, that it was written at a period when a French invasion was expected. It is a very hard and difficult thing for us in the present day, broken as we are into so many factions, to conceive the united enthusiasm which stirred the heart of England in those days, when every moment the invasion of the great conqueror of Europe was possible. The fleets of England swept the seas; on every hill the signal beacons blazed; 420,000 men were in arms; the service of the church was liable to be interrupted by the clang of arms upon the pavement; every village churchyard was converted into a parade-ground; every boy felt as if there were strength, even in his puny arm, to strike a blow in defence of the cause of his country; every man, excepting when he thought of the women of his country, was longing for the time to come, when it should be seen with what a strength, with what a majesty a soldier fought, when he was fighting in the magnificent and awful cause of his altar and his hearth.

The moment was like that of the deep silence which precedes a thunder-storm, when every breath is hushed, and every separate dried leaf, as it falls through the boughs, is heard tinkling tinkling down through the branches, from branch to branch; when men's breath was held; when men's blood beat thick in their hearts, as if they were waiting in solemn and grand, but

not in painful—rather in triumphant—expecta-
tion for the moment when the storm should
break, and the French cry of "Glory" should
be thundered back again by England's sublimer
battle-cry of "Duty!" It was at this time
that Wordsworth's sonnet appeared:—

> "It is not to be thought of that the flood
>   Of British freedom, which to the open sea
>   Of the world's praise, from dark antiquity
>   Hath flowed, with 'pomp of waters unwithstood,'
>   Roused though it be full often to a mood
>   Which spurns the check of salutary bands,
>   That this most famous stream in bogs and sands
>   Should perish! and to evil and to good
>   Be lost for ever.   In our halls is hung
> Armoury of the invincible Knights of old :
> We must be free or die, who speak the tongue
> That Shakspeare spake ; the faith and morals hold
> Which Milton held.   In everything we are sprung
> Of earth's first blood, have titles manifold."

In the next passage I have to bring before
you I will remind you of some other facts.
The sonnet is addressed to the men of Kent.
Now, there is a difference between the Kentish
men and the men of Kent.   The Kentish men
are simply the inhabitants of the county of
Kent.   The "Men of Kent" is a technical expression applied to the inhabitants of that part
of Kent who were never subdued in the
Norman invasion, and who obtained glorious
terms for themselves, on capitulation, receiving
the confirmation of their own charters ; so that

until very recently—if not at present—they
were still in possession of the custom called
Gavelkind, by which the sons inherited, not
unequally, the eldest taking precedence, but
they all taking share and share alike. It was
to the " Men of Kent," the inhabitants of that
part of the county nearest to the neighbouring
land of France, that Wordsworth addressed
this sonnet :—

> " Vanguard of Liberty, ye Men of Kent,
>   Ye children of a soil that doth advance
>   Her haughty brow against the coast of France,
>   Now is the time to prove your hardiment !
>   To France be words of invitation sent !
>   They from their fields can see the countenance
>   Of your fierce war, may ken the glittering lance,
>   And hear you shouting forth your brave intent.
>   Left single, in bold parley, ye, of yore,
>   Did from the Norman win a gallant wreath ;
>   Confirmed the charters that were yours before ;
>   No parleying now !   In Britain is one breath,
>   We all are with you now from shore to shore :—
>   Ye men of Kent, 'tis victory or death ! "

In this age of cosmopolitanism, when we are,
forsooth, too much philanthropists to be
patriots ; when any deep and strong emotion
of love to our country is reckoned as nothing
more than the sacredness of the schoolboy's
affection ; when our young people who have
travelled can find no words more capable of
expressing their contempt than these—" It is so
English ; " it does the heart good to read these

firm and pure, and true and manly words, issuing from the lips of one who was not ashamed to love his country with all his heart, and with all his soul, and with all his mind, and with all his strength : a man whose every word, and every thought, and every act, were the words and thoughts, and acts, of a manly, true-spirited, high-minded Englishman !